Praise for
Beauty Begins

"In *Beauty Begins,* Chris Shook and Megan Shook Alpha have written a vibrant, heartwarming book for women of all ages who live out the universal struggle to see themselves as beautiful. Through their personal stories, biblical insight, and practical wisdom, this mother-daughter duo gives us down-to-earth advice on how to see ourselves clearly through God's eyes of acceptance and love. I can't wait to share it with my granddaughters!"

> —KAY WARREN, cofounder of Saddleback Church
> with her husband, Rick; international speaker;
> and best-selling author of *Choose Joy: Because
> Happiness Isn't Enough*

"In an age of superficial beauty and supermodel icons, our friends Chris and Megan offer a Christ-centered alternative that begins with the heart of God. Here's a wise and wonderful guide to where true beauty begins—and to the confidence and contentment that come from it."

> —LEE AND LESLIE STROBEL, authors of *Surviving
> a Spiritual Mismatch in Marriage*

"True beauty begins when you make peace with your reflection. That's why Chris Shook and her daughter, Megan, have taken the risk to talk about a topic that is often difficult for women to discuss—self-image. The result is an invitation for ladies of all ages to join this conversation."

—Pastor Steven and Holly Furtick, cofounders
of Elevation Church, Charlotte, NC

"Beauty in the eyes of the world is distorted. In *Beauty Begins,* Chris Shook and her daughter, Megan, point women of all ages to the source of true beauty: the heart of God. They reveal that God's heart is for women to be full of beauty, full of joy, full of peace. Let Chris and Megan clear your vision and teach you the truth of who God made you to be."

—Matthew Barnett, cofounder of the Dream
Center and author of *God's Dream for You*

Beauty Begins

Beauty Begins

MAKING PEACE WITH YOUR REFLECTION

CHRIS SHOOK &
MEGAN SHOOK ALPHA

WATERBROOK
PRESS

Beauty Begins
Published by WaterBrook Press
12265 Oracle Boulevard, Suite 200
Colorado Springs, Colorado 80921

This book is not intended to replace the medical advice of a trained medical professional. Readers are advised to consult a physician or other qualified health-care professional regarding treatment of their medical problems. The author and publisher specifically disclaim liability, loss, or risk, personal or otherwise, which is incurred as a consequence, directly or indirectly, of the use or application of any of the contents of this book.

All Scripture quotations, unless otherwise indicated, are taken from the Holy Bible, New International Version®, NIV®. Copyright © 1973, 1978, 1984, 2011 by Biblica Inc.® Used by permission. All rights reserved worldwide. Scripture quotations marked (ESV) are taken from the ESV® Bible (the Holy Bible, English Standard Version®), copyright © 2001 by Crossway, a publishing ministry of Good News Publishers. Used by permission. All rights reserved. Scripture quotations marked (KJV) are taken from the King James Version. Scripture quotations marked (TLB) are taken from The Living Bible copyright © 1971. Used by permission of Tyndale House Publishers Inc., Carol Stream, Illinois 60188. All rights reserved. Scripture quotations marked (MSG) are taken from the Message. Copyright © by Eugene H. Peterson 1993, 1994, 1995, 1996, 2000, 2001, 2002. Used by permission of Tyndale House Publishers Inc. Scripture quotations marked (NASB) are taken from the New American Standard Bible®. Copyright © 1960, 1962, 1963, 1968, 1971, 1972, 1973, 1975, 1977, 1995 by the Lockman Foundation. Used by permission. (www .Lockman.org). Scripture quotations marked (NIrV) are taken from the Holy Bible, New International Reader's Version®. NIrV®. Copyright © 1995, 1996, 1998 by Biblica Inc.® Used by permission. All rights reserved worldwide. Scripture quotations marked (NKJV) are taken from the New King James Version®. Copyright © 1982 by Thomas Nelson Inc. Used by permission. All rights reserved. Scripture quotations marked (NLT) are taken from the Holy Bible, New Living Translation, copyright © 1996, 2004, 2007, 2013 by Tyndale House Foundation. Used by permission of Tyndale House Publishers Inc., Carol Stream, Illinois 60188. All rights reserved.

Hardcover ISBN 978-1-60142-729-8
eBook ISBN 978-1-60142-731-1

Copyright © 2016 by Chris Shook and Megan Shook

Cover design by Shane Caskey

Published in the United States by WaterBrook Multnomah, an imprint of the Crown Publishing Group, a division of Penguin Random House LLC, New York.

WaterBrook® and its deer colophon are registered trademarks of Penguin Random House LLC.

Library of Congress Cataloging-in-Publication Data
Names: Shook, Chris, author. | Shook Alpha, Megan, author.
Title: Beauty begins : making peace with your reflection / Chris Shook and Megan Shook Alpha.
Description: First edition. | Colorado Springs, Colorado : WaterBrook Press, [2016] | Includes bibliographical references.
Identifiers: LCCN 2015043075 (print) | LCCN 2015044591 (ebook) | ISBN 9781601427298 (hardcover) | ISBN 9781601427311 (electronic)
Subjects: LCSH: Christian women—Religious life. | Mothers and daughters—Religious aspects—Christianity. | Self-perception—Religious aspects—Christianity. | Beauty, Personal—Religious aspects—Christianity.
Classification: LCC BV4527 .S434 2016 (print) | LCC BV4527 (ebook) | DDC 248.8/43—dc23
LC record available at http://lccn.loc.gov/2015043075

Printed in the United States of America
2016

10 9 8 7 6 5 4 3 2

This book is dedicated to all the women who encourage us when we stumble, cheer for us when we succeed, and challenge us when we get too comfortable. We love doing life with you!

Nancy. Lisa. Sarah. Kelli. Shelley. Mary. Alice. Annette. Cassi. Janet. Emily. Sandy. Molly. Kathy. Allison. Eileen. Abby. Karen. Edie. Brandi. Brittany. Tammy. Jen. Susan. Heather. Pattie. Jackie. Rainey. Chaundel. Alex. Sue. Haley. Hazel. Paige. Caroline. Bindu. Jodi. Vivi-Anne.

Contents

Contents

Note To The Reader

This book is unique in two ways. First, this book was written by a mother and daughter. Second, it is designed for girls and women of all ages. We address struggles that all women deal with daily, and we also explore the unique relationship between mothers and daughters.

In our society it is impossible not to feel inadequate at times. It's hard to make it through even one day without feeling insecure about ourselves! As a mother and daughter living in the same hurting world you live in, we will share our struggles, our joys, and how we have learned to embrace this tough yet rewarding life. We aren't saying we have figured it all out, but we have discovered some practical ways to love the person God made us to be.

As mother and daughter we've shared many of the experiences described in this book. For simplicity *we* has become *I* in the writing except for a few instances when clarification was necessary. Regardless of your age or life stage, we believe the ideas we present will resonate in your heart.

The main thing we want you to know is that it is never too late for beauty to begin in *your* life.

The Beautiful Truth

You shall know the truth, and the truth shall make you free.

—John 8:32, nkjv

God cannot give us a happiness and peace apart from Himself, because it is not there. There is no such thing.

—C. S. Lewis

1

The Distorted Reflection

Beauty Begins in the Heart of God

He has made everything beautiful in its time.

—ECCLESIASTES 3:11

We are so accustomed to disguise ourselves to others that in the end we become disguised to ourselves.

—FRANÇOIS DE LA ROCHEFOUCAULD

Do you feel beautiful? It's a simple, straightforward question. But it may be one of the most significant, revealing questions you could ever answer.

I'm not talking about all the cliché answers to the question. I'm not interested in how you *think* you should answer the question. What I'm really asking is, "How do you feel about your reflection?" When you look in the mirror, what is the first emotion that hits you? Is it a feeling of complete contentment? Does your reflection fill you with a deep sense of peace or a deep sense of inadequacy? I mean, most of the time do you feel beautiful?

I think the majority of women, if we're completely honest, would admit that we don't feel beautiful much of the time. Recently our women's ministry team at Woodlands Church surveyed hundreds of young women and asked this question: "If you could change anything about the way you look, would you?" More than 70 percent of them answered yes and went on to name all the things they would change. We also asked, "On a scale of one to ten, how beautiful do you think you are, with one being 'I can't think of anything I like about myself' and ten being 'I am completely content.'" Only 11 percent of the girls said, "I'm completely content and at peace with my reflection."

The vast majority of young ladies who took the survey are committed Christians who are very involved in church and have great friends. I have found, however, that this struggle to feel beautiful is almost as prevalent among Christian women as it is among non-Christian women. The truth is, almost every woman battles to feel beautiful every single day. Most of us have never made peace with our reflections.

STEALING BEAUTY

Making peace with your reflection is so important, because if you fail to do that, you will declare war on yourself! Generations of women have become casualties in this war on self-worth. The battle to feel beautiful has contributed to everything from low self-esteem and poor body image to eating disorders and self-harm.

- Ninety-one percent of women surveyed on a college campus had attempted to control their weight through dieting; 22 percent dieted "often" or "always."[1]
- Eighty-six percent of young women reported the onset of an eating disorder by age twenty; 43 percent reported the onset between the ages of sixteen and twenty.[2]
- Anorexia is the third most common chronic illness among adolescents.[3]
- Ninety-five percent of those who have eating disorders are between the ages of twelve and twenty-five.[4]
- Twenty-five percent of college-aged women engage in bingeing and purging as a weight-management technique.[5]
- The mortality rate associated with anorexia nervosa is twelve times higher than the death rate associated with all other causes of death for females fifteen to twenty-four years old.[6]

We need to wake up and realize we have a dangerous enemy who has declared war on us. Jesus tells us in the gospel of John that our enemy, Satan, has a purpose for our lives.

The thief comes only to steal and kill and destroy;
I have come that they may have life, and have it to
the full. (John 10:10)

Jesus warns us that Satan is a thief whose strategy is to steal our self-worth, kill our passion for life, and destroy our hopes and dreams.

On the other hand, Christ has come not to *steal* our self-worth but to *fill* our self-worth. Christ has come to give us "life . . . to the full," and that means He wants us to feel full of beauty, full of joy, full of peace, and full of value and meaning!

The Bible also lets us know the first step in the Enemy's strategy to steal our true beauty. He always starts with a lie. In the gospel of John, chapter 8, Jesus tells us that Satan is "a liar and the father of lies" (verse 44).

The world's oldest liar gets us to forget that we were
God's idea in the first place. We don't always remember
that there is a very real God on a very real throne who
calls us His beloved. The slithering enemy convinces us
that our Maker's love is never enough, never was. And
Satan continually asks us to consider what others are
thinking of us.[7]
—Jennifer Dukes Lee

Satan will constantly whisper destructive lies in your thoughts. They go something like this: "You're not beautiful. You're not valuable. You're not worth anything." Then he gets really specific with his lies. "You're too fat." "You're too tall." "You're too short." "Your hair is too dull." "Your nose is too big." "Your lips are too small." "Your eyes aren't the right color." And the lies go on and on.

It's all lies! If you start to believe the lies, you will base your actions and decisions on a foundation of lies and never discover your true beauty.

But Jesus tells us the truth will set us free (see John 8:32). When we begin to believe the truth of who we really are and who God made us to be, we'll be set free to feel beautiful. Our goal in writing *Beauty Begins* is to encourage all of us to stop believing the lies and to start living the truth. To be honest, we're tired of watching a generation of beautiful young girls and women, along with their mothers, being slowly and methodically destroyed by the lies of Satan that our culture constantly tries to force on us. So let's start with a dose of truth about what beauty really is.

Beauty begins in the heart of God, and He placed that longing for beauty in our hearts. The problem is that our culture presents a distorted view of true beauty. When we look in the broken mirror of our culture long enough, we start to believe the distorted reflection is reality.

BEAUTIFUL VERSUS PRETTY

Would you rather be described as beautiful or pretty?

Our culture has completely confused the meaning of true beauty with the concept of pretty. There's a huge difference between beautiful and pretty. Sociologists tell us that *beauty* is defined differently, depending on the culture. I know what they are saying, but I think it's *pretty* that means different things in different cultures. Humanity's idea about what is pretty changes from culture to culture and is constantly changing within cultures.

It's eye opening to take a quick skip back through history and look at the preferred shapes for women. In the Middle Ages a woman was considered pretty if she was large and pale, and she was considered very unattractive if she was thin and tan. If a woman was heavy and pale, it meant she was part of the aristocracy and had plenty of food to eat and didn't have to work in the fields in the hot sun.

Pretty in the early nineteen hundreds was a woman who was buxom and had curvy hips. The 1920s liked a trim figure that looked good in those short flapper dresses. Like the stock market, hemlines fell in the '30s, and curvy shapes returned. This intensified in the '40s as voluptuous was the shape to welcome home war heroes. And that shape reached a zenith in the '50s. Think Marilyn Monroe.

The '60s saw the miniskirt. The '70s and '80s were just strange. The '90s presented the waif—popular but not healthy. And the early part of the twenty-first century promoted extreme exercise and dieting and a shape hard to attain.[8]

As the new millennium progresses, our culture's view of pretty will continue to change, and each change has the potential to reshape the way we see ourselves—probably not for the better.

What will the future hold for the preferred shape for women? If history tells us anything, it's that trends don't last long. Pretty is an ever-changing illusion that enslaves women and girls to fashion, diets, and gym memberships. Most of all, it keeps us in a constant state of discontent. The airbrushed, manipulated images in today's magazines leave women and girls feeling hopelessly inadequate by comparison.

Fashion, styles, and what we consider pretty constantly change. Beauty on the other hand is universal and never changes. Recently I (Chris) was driving home from the grocery store. As I rounded the corner, I was stopped in my tracks by real beauty. I had to pull the car over because I was looking at the most amazing sunset I had ever seen in my life. It was absolutely stunning with every color you can imagine—oranges and yellows, pinks, purples, and blues. It was so incredible I just sat there in awe taking it all in. Immediately I thought, *Anybody in the entire world who saw this sunset would do what I'm doing—watching with wonder and amazement.* In any country, in any culture, at any age, any person on the planet would recognize the beauty of the sunset.

Why is that? Why in different cultures do we find different things to be pretty, and yet something about raw, wild beauty transcends our differences?

As I watched that sunset, it hit me. I saw it so clearly that for a brief moment it was as if I was no longer looking through the distorted mirror of our culture. I realized that real beauty begins with God. Therefore, something is beautiful because it has God's fingerprints all over it.

I couldn't look at the brilliantly colored canvas of that evening sky without seeing the hand of the Master Artist who painted it.

THE FINGERPRINTS OF THE MASTER ARTIST

If you walk through an art museum and see the beautiful paintings of the masters like Monet, Rembrandt, Renoir, and Michelangelo, you wouldn't think, *I guess someone spilled a bucket of paint on that canvas.* No, you would immediately recognize that it was painted by a master artist. The fingerprints of the master artist are all over it. That's what it was like when I looked at that sunset.

In all our lives there are moments when we catch a glimpse

of raw, real beauty. It's like a door that's slightly open, allowing bright light to come through. We see a little crack of light, and for a second we remember what beautiful really is.

We remember what we were created for. We remember that the One who created that sunset also created you and me. We remember that we are beautiful.

Then we forget again. We forget who created us. We forget whom we are trying to please. We forget what real beauty is.

Do you believe God sees you as beautiful? You'll begin to feel beautiful when you start believing the truth that the Master Artist beautifully created you.

Imagine a famous painter, some fiery Italian known for his impeccably high standards. Imagine the artist has been working on a particular canvas for years. The rumor around town is that this project will be his magnum opus, his great work. You know that a creative work that's worth anything demands the artist pour himself fully into the work. You consider all the planning and effort, the sleepless nights and grueling days that have gone into this special creation.

Finally one day a child runs through the streets of town shouting, "It is finished! It is finished!" Everyone heads toward the artist's house for the grand unveiling. But before the crowd gets a chance to see it, the artist steps back from the canvas to make his personal critique first. He stands there almost spellbound, taking in every color, every brush stroke, every nuance of shade and texture—everything. A tear comes to his eye as his mouth breaks into a smile, and he speaks aloud only two words: *"Molto bello!"* Very beautiful!

Something similar happened in Genesis when God unveiled His greatest creation. Far from a cold, distant watchmaker who turned a key and set everything in motion, God, as He is described in Genesis, is a very personal God who went to great pains to speak into existence and to fashion all that is, including us. When He was finished, He was infinitely pleased with the outcome. In fact, He was so pleased that He decided to stop. Nothing more was needed. No more tweaks or revisions.

The Master Artist created you and said, "You are beautiful, my child!"

But we've believed the lies of the Enemy. We've looked away from the mirror of God's truth, and we've looked in the distorted mirror of our culture. We've broken away from the God who beautifully created us and loves us completely. Because we've broken away from God, we've become broken in the ugliness of our sins and failures.

THE TRUE REFLECTION

But here's the great news! God can take even our brokenness and turn it into beauty.

That's why real beauty begins at the Cross. God took the

ugliest event in all history and turned it into the most beautiful act in all history. On the cross Christ took our ugliest sins, mistakes, and failures and replaced them with the beauty of forgiveness, purpose, and—one day—heaven. That's where beauty begins.

Beauty begins in a love that never ends!

I want you to know that I don't have it all together. I struggle just as you do to live in the truth that I'm beautiful. As we start this journey together to make peace with our reflections, I encourage you to put this scripture on your mirror and look at it every time you see yourself. The writer of Psalm 45 directs our attention to the mirror of truth.

> Listen, daughter, and pay careful attention:
>> Forget your people and your father's house.
> Let the king be enthralled by your beauty;
>> honor him, for he is your lord. (verses 10–11)

I've had this verse on my mirror and on my desk for years because it reminds me that God is "enthralled" by my beauty! I like how the psalmist speaks directly to the bride: "Listen, daughter, and pay careful attention." He's saying, "Stop listening to the lies and listen to the truth! Stop looking at the distorted mirror of the culture, and look into the eyes of your King!"

The King of kings is "enthralled" by your beauty too. He is so enthralled with you that He gave up His throne in heaven to come into our broken world and win you over to Himself.

As we travel this road toward recognizing and living from our true beauty, I encourage you to spend time every day in God's Word. At the end of each chapter is a Reflection page followed by a scripture I want you to meditate on.

As we constantly look in the mirror of truth, we'll see our sacred reflections more clearly, and we'll reflect the beauty of Christ to others more consistently.

Reflection

1. Make a list of beautiful traits you would like to build into your character.

2. Read Psalm 45:10–11 again: "Listen, daughter, and pay careful attention: Forget your people and your father's house. Let the king be enthralled by your beauty; honor him, for he is your lord." Think about the truth that the God who created you is enthralled by your beauty. Write that verse on a note card or a Post-it Note, and put it on your mirror to remind yourself how beautiful you truly are.

Prayer

Lord, thank You for making me beautiful. I need Your help to remember that truth each day and to share it with others. The lies of the Enemy are so strong in our culture that it's easy to forget the truth of who I am. I know real beauty begins in You, and You alone. You are the Master Artist of summer sunsets and classic symphonies and Christmas snow and me. Thank You. Amen.

Listen, daughter, and pay careful attention:
  Forget your people and your father's house.
Let the **king** be **enthralled** by your beauty;
  honor **him**, for he is your lord.

PSALM 45:10–11

2

The Mirror Addiction

Beauty Begins with My Sacred Reflection

Do not love this world nor the things it
offers you, for when you love the world, you
do not have the love of the Father in you.

—1 John 2:15, nlt

We are mirrors whose brightness . . . is
wholly derived from the sun that shines
upon us.

—C. S. Lewis

How many times a day do you look in the mirror? Women have a love-hate relationship with mirrors. We seem to be drawn to them the way a mosquito is drawn to a bug zapper. We can't seem to stay away from mirrors, but we rarely love what they reflect back to us. On the rare occasion we really like our reflections, we still come back to the mirror quickly to make sure everything is still in place.

This addiction to mirrors is like every other harmful addiction. It's the result of trying to meet a God-given need with the wrong thing.

AM I BEAUTIFUL?

Each of us was born with a sacred reflection, what I like to call our "truest self." So we have a divine desire, which God placed inside us, to constantly look for our sacred reflections. If we catch a glimpse of them, everything changes.

In the familiar fairy tale and classic Disney movie *Snow White and the Seven Dwarfs*, we see an example of the mirror addiction. Snow White's evil stepmother routinely asks the now-famous question of her magic mirror: "Who's the fairest of them all?" Of course the answer always affirms the queen. That is until the fateful day when Snow White has grown up and the mirror has to tell the queen the truth, that there is one who is "more fair than thee."

> Little girls want to know, Am I lovely? The twirling
> skirts, the dress up, the longing to be pretty and to be
> seen—that is what that's all about. We are seeking an
> answer to our Question.[9]
> —John and Stasi Eldredge

The mirror's revelation sets in motion the envy of the queen, the mercy of the huntsman, the friendship of the dwarfs, the poison apple, and you know how it goes from there. But it all began with a woman asking the right question to the wrong kind of mirror.

Am I fair? Am I beautiful? It's actually an honest and God-inspired question. But we must be careful whom we ask.

The problem comes when we look in the wrong mirror for our answer.

HOUSE OF MIRRORS

When I (Megan) was a little girl, my dad took me to a county fair. It was one of those sketchy little carnivals where you can get about every fried food imaginable and risk your life on crazy rides that were assembled just the day before! One of the attractions was called the House of Mirrors. In actuality it was a simple hallway lined with distorted mirrors. Some made me look several feet taller, and others made me look really short and squatty. Some mirrors made my face appear huge, while others made my nose grow like Pinocchio's. All the mirrors in the House of Mirrors distorted my reflection.

You and I were made to look for our sacred reflections. But we keep looking in mirrors that distort our reflections.

Now we see things imperfectly as in a poor mirror,
but then we will see everything with perfect clarity.

All that I know now is partial and incomplete, but
then I will know everything completely, just as God
knows me now. (1 Corinthians 13:12, NLT 1996)

We were made to look in the mirror. We've just been looking in the wrong mirrors.

We were made to look in the mirror of Christ's love to see
our sacred reflections. But as 1 Corinthians 13:12 says, we look
in a lot of poor mirrors here on earth.

THE MIRROR OF PARENTS

The first mirror we look in is the mirror in our parents' eyes.
Children's first concept of who they are comes from looking
into the eyes of their parents and seeing what is reflected back
to them. If you looked into the eyes of a parent and saw value,
love, and beauty reflected back to you, then chances are good
you grew up feeling valued and beautiful. But if you looked into
a parent's eyes and saw stress, anxiety, and distraction reflected
back, then you probably grew up feeling insecure. If you constantly saw a critical look from a parent, then it's likely you feel
as if you don't measure up.

I see this destructive pattern repeated over and over with
moms and daughters. Insecure girls grow up to be insecure

mothers. A daughter sees her beautiful mother—the most important and loved person in her world—looking critically at herself in the mirror. Then mom voices her insecurities. "I look fat. My hips are too wide. I hate my complexion." And if this is repeated day after day, week after week, then the conclusion the little girl draws is "If mom doesn't like the way she looks, then I must not be beautiful either."

> If you want to understand any woman you
> must first ask about her mother and then listen
> carefully.[10]
>   —Anita Diamant

The mirror of Mom is one of the most powerful—and unfortunately often one of the most distorted—mirrors in a daughter's life.

Here's the deal. In a sense we all grew up in a house of mirrors because there are no perfect parents. Even with the best of parents, there is some distortion in their mirrors, because none of us has it all together. We'll talk later in the book about really important things moms and dads can do to help show God's sacred reflection to a daughter. But ultimately the sacred reflection can only be found in the eyes of our perfect heavenly Father.

THE MIRROR OF PEERS

As a young girl moves into her teen years, the mirror of her mother is often replaced by the mirror of peers as the primary source she looks to most days. When she looks in the mirror of friends, she may see reflected back one of two extremes—"I hate myself" or "I love myself too much."

Let me explain what I mean. During the day I constantly compare myself to other women, and I think, *Wow, I am so fat! Why don't I look like her? Why can't I just stop thinking about food for a second and have some self-control? Ugh! I need to go to the gym and work out. I'm never going to look better.* Or I think, *Good thing I'm not as fat as she is. Look at that girl. I look so much better than she does. Well, at least I'm not like her!* I am so embarrassed to tell you I think that way! But I am telling you because I know you can relate. I know you have put yourself down, and I know you have put others down to feel as if you aren't worthless. Neither of these approaches is the right way to think about ourselves, but trying to change our thought process and our sense of self-worth is incredibly hard. It's not "Just do these three things, and you will instantly feel good about yourself and the way you look and who you are!" Nope. It just doesn't work like that.

First we have to stop looking in all the distorted mirrors and instead look in the mirror of Christ's love. When we look in the mirror of Christ's love, we discover our sacred reflections, and we see mirrored back complete love, beauty, and acceptance. When we look in this mirror, we start to believe the truth that all girls are equally beautiful. Even though our flesh might tell us that is not true, Christ's eyes tell us that it is. We are all equally beautiful in His eyes, not one girl more stunning or more amazing than another. We look different and are different sizes, but that's because God chose for us to be different.

We forget this truth when we start to think, *God didn't give me this body. He gave me a normal-sized body, and I ruined it and became ugly.* I know you've had that thought because those are the lies that run through my mind when I look in the mirror or when I see someone whose body appears to be better than mine.

Maybe you have gained some weight or something about your appearance isn't as attractive as it used to be. That does not make you any less beautiful to God. His love for you is complete and unconditional. There is nothing you can do to make God love you any more or any less than He does right now. When you mess up and sin, it hurts Him because He knows how devastating sin is in your life and relationships. But He doesn't love you any less. And when you obey Him and do good things, He doesn't love you more. He can't love you more than He already does because He loves you perfectly and completely!

THE MIRROR THAT MATTERS

What I'm saying is, the only mirror that matters is God's, which is easier said than believed and lived out, but it's true. That doesn't mean it's okay not to take care of our bodies and habitually overeat or eat unhealthy foods. The Bible says we should treat our bodies as God's temples, which means taking care of them. Yes, we should exercise and eat well and get adequate rest. But that doesn't mean we have to be on a strict diet and never eat goodies or take a break from working out.

The truth is that it's not about us. We need to stop focusing on ourselves so much and what we look like, what we eat, what we wear, whether we look better than the girl walking by, and what other people think of us. We have to *just stop*!

> Let's just go ahead and be what we were made to be,
> without enviously or pridefully comparing ourselves
> with each other, or trying to be something we aren't.
> (Romans 12:6, MSG)

We have to stop looking in the mirror of culture, the mirror of parents, and the mirror of peers. We have to start looking in the only mirror where we'll find our sacred reflections. Hebrews 12:1–2 tells us where to look: "Let us run with perseverance the race marked out for us, fixing our eyes on Jesus, the pioneer and perfecter of faith. For the joy set before him he endured the cross."

The only mirror where we can see our true and sacred reflections is the eyes of Christ. The writer of Hebrews tells us that beauty begins at the Cross when he says that Christ endured the cross because of the "joy set before him." What was the joy set before Him? It was *you*! And it was *me*!

As He hung on the cross, He was thinking about you. The joy of knowing that His death would bring you life and restore your relationship with Him gave Christ the strength to endure the cross.

When you look into the eyes of Christ, you'll see reflected back beauty, worth, love, value, and meaning. When you look into the eyes of Christ, you will see your sacred reflection. Once you get a glimpse of your sacred reflection, you will start to reflect the beauty of Christ to others.

ETERNAL BEAUTY

Have you ever been told that you resemble someone? Maybe people say, "You have your dad's eyes" or "You have your mom's nose" or "You have your grandpa's chin."

Genesis tells us that we were created in the image of God. Therefore, we have the capacity to be in a relationship with Him. The more we grow in that relationship with Christ, the more we resemble Him and reflect His image to the people around us.

Where does your life look like Christ's? That is where you are beautiful. That is the source of your true beauty. It's from being like Christ. We are always trying to imitate other people instead of imitating God. But the more we reflect Christlike character to the people around us, the more beautiful we'll feel.

Therefore be imitators of God, as beloved children; and walk in love, just as Christ also loved you and gave Himself up for us, an offering and a sacrifice to God as a fragrant aroma. (Ephesians 5:1–2, NASB)

This passage tells us the One we are to imitate is God. God is not some cosmic being who created the universe and then left us without an example to follow. No, He put on human flesh and came to this earth so we could see true beauty up close and personal. When we look at Christ's life, we see what God is like and what beauty really looks like.

The more we become like Christ in our character, the more beautiful we become. The most beautiful people I've known are those whose character most resembles Christ's. The character qualities of Jesus—love, mercy, grace, wisdom, patience, peace, and kindness—are reflected from their souls.

One of the biggest differences between pretty and beautiful

relates to time. Beauty is eternal, while pretty is always temporary. It's important to take care of our bodies and to pursue a healthy lifestyle, but we have to remember our bodies are temporary. I have a friend who calls our bodies our "earth suits" because we need them only here on earth. Scripture says we'll get new, heavenly bodies when we leave this earth. Our earthly bodies aren't eternal. Only our character lasts forever.

We spend so much time trying to make our temporary bodies look good, but we spend very little time making sure our eternal character is beautiful. God is much more interested in our character than our comfort. That's why He'll push us out of our comfort zones into His character-building zone.

The two ways God changes our character to reflect Him are through the Bible and through problems. In chapter 4 we'll talk more about how He uses problems and pain to make us beautiful, but first I want you to awaken to the beauty of truth in God's Word. The more time we spend looking at the mirror of truth in God's Word, the easier it is for us to recognize the distorted mirror of Satan's lies.

Remember you are beautiful because of the Cross! There was nothing pretty about Christ's death on the cross. But it was beautiful! His act of forgiveness, sacrifice, and love for us is beautiful because it is eternal and never changing. Look in the mirror of that beautiful truth today, and see your beautiful reflection in the eyes of the One who gave Himself up for you.

Reflection

1. What distorted mirror do you look in the most? How does it affect the way you feel about yourself? Every time you look in the mirror, remind yourself that the only mirror that matters is the eyes of Christ reflecting back your true beauty.

2. Read Ephesians 5:1–2 (NASB) again: "Therefore be imitators of God, as beloved children; and walk in love, just as Christ also loved you and gave Himself up for us, an offering and a sacrifice to God as a fragrant aroma." Think about the friends or fashion trends you've tried to imitate over the years. Now list the areas of your life in which you need to look more like Christ, and ask God to shine His beauty through you to others.

Prayer

Lord, like every woman, I want to know "Am I lovely?"
So many mirrors in my life seek to tell me the answer
to that question. But I know the only mirror that really
matters is Yours. I praise You for my sacred reflection,
and I pray that I can reflect Your beauty to others as
I grow to look more like You. Amen.

Let's just go ahead and **be** what we were **made to be**, without enviously or pridefully comparing ourselves with each other, or trying to be something we aren't.

Romans 12:6, MSG

3

The Selfie Obsession

Beauty Begins Where Self Ends

Fancy hairstyles don't make you beautiful. Wearing gold jewelry or fine clothes doesn't make you beautiful. Instead, your beauty comes from inside you. It is the beauty of a gentle and quiet spirit. Beauty like this doesn't fade away. God places great value on it.

—1 Peter 3:3–4, NIrV

Too often we underestimate the power of a touch, a smile, a kind word, a listening ear, an honest compliment, or the smallest act of caring, all of which have the potential to turn a life around.

—Leo Buscaglia

We are constantly told in our culture that beauty begins with us, that beauty is found in the clothes we wear, the makeup we put on, the shape of our bodies, the color of our hair, the muscle tone in our arms. And that's just the tip of the iceberg. When we believe the lie that beauty begins with us, then we look for our reflections in the bathroom mirror. We become overly concerned with our outward appearance and not as concerned about the needs of others.

The paradox is that when we focus on outward appearance, we turn inward and become self-centered. But when we focus on inner beauty, we become outward focused and less selfish.

Beauty doesn't begin with us. Beauty begins with God. When you look for your sacred reflection in Christ's eyes, you'll find yourself looking in your mirror a lot less.

THE "I" MONSTER

Beauty begins where self ends. When we stop focusing on ourselves, even for a second, we realize we aren't the only people on the planet! When we get caught up in ourselves and how we look, our whole world hangs on whether we work out, eat healthy food, feel good, look good, or are at our ideal weight. We turn into I monsters. If we are not satisfied with ourselves, then we are more likely to be upset and feel our day is ruined. Think for a minute how truly selfish that sounds. When we starve ourselves, work out a lot, and focus on ourselves, we think we will look and feel better, but just the opposite occurs.

This focus on self becomes self-destructive.

Many young women struggle with eating disorders that stem from the distorted mirror of our culture that says we need to look a certain way to be beautiful. Our culture says if we don't look like the stick-thin, airbrushed, enhanced pictures of the supermodels in magazines, then we aren't beautiful. That's a lie! A great big, destructive lie because it takes our focus off the mirror of God's truth and puts it on the mirrors in our bathrooms. The focus then becomes self, and as I said, that's self-destructive.

I realize there is much more to eating disorders and similar problems than just a self-focus. Chemical imbalances and deep psychological, emotional, and spiritual issues may be involved. In all our destructive habits, however, there is an element of self-centeredness. We can get so caught up in *How do I feel?* and *How do I look?* and *What is everyone thinking about me?* that in our heads the whole world revolves around us rather than God.

When I'm really down on my outward appearance, I have to admit I'm focusing on myself rather than on God and others. I'm not saying that we should totally ignore our appearance or that it's horribly evil to fix our hair, wear jewelry, or put on a nice outfit. No, we just need to realize that none of this is going to make us beautiful or feed our souls. The answer to beauty is not outer appearance, because that's not the source of beauty.

THE GREAT LIE: GOD'S NOT ENOUGH

Scarcity. The first and greatest lie. And the spin the serpent put on it in the garden was not "Eve, you're not enough" but "God's not enough for you, Eve. You're really on your own. Reach out and grab all you can, because everything's on your shoulders. No one is looking out for you."

We might act as though everything is fine, but rarely a day goes by when we don't compare ourselves to other women. Like water dripping on a rock, this constant pressure of comparison has worn us down. We are always striving to be like someone else in some way. If we all looked and acted the same, there would be nothing to compare. But God intentionally made us all different according to His plan. We each fill a purpose. Imagine how boring and nonproductive our world would be if we were all the same!

I know that longing to be wanted, to be loved and cherished. Every woman in the world, Christian or not, feels this way because that is how God designed us. We long for intimacy with someone. We long for security, to know that everything is going to be okay and that we will be taken care of. We all desire that emptiness in us to be filled. We all want to be loved.

One of our greatest fears is that no one will want us. We compensate by trying to be liked by everyone, especially men, which makes it easy for us to stumble into sin. We try to fill that void on our own. When we realize we aren't getting as much attention as we want, we change ourselves for people so they will pay attention to us. We want to feel adored, so we wear revealing clothes to get guys' attention. We want to feel wanted, so we give in to sexual temptation and hand our bodies over to others. We want to feel important, so we put others down to feel better about ourselves. We want to be known, so we change ourselves to fit the mold of our broken society, all so that some-one might notice us. All this stems from our searching for love in the wrong places and looking in distorted mirrors for our sacred reflections.

When we feel we don't have control of our lives, we find something, like food, that we can control, and it starts to take over. The problem is that we are trying to take control of our lives when we should be giving control to God.

We all have struggles, but they can't control our lives if we let God take control first. Jesus told us, "In this world you will have trouble. But take heart! I have overcome the world" (John 16:33). Will it still be hard? Yes! Will you still be tempted? Of course! We don't get to choose what we struggle with, but we do get to decide how to deal with those struggles.

We're all afflicted with self-obsession to some degree, so don't let this idea overwhelm you. Instead, look at this realiza-tion as an opportunity. This broken world is filled with billions of opportunities to take your focus off yourself. It is not about thinking less of yourself but thinking *about* yourself less and others more.

THE GREAT TRUTH

You probably have received credit-card offers in the mail. On the front of the envelope, they usually say you have been "preapproved" for the card. What if I told you that it works the same way with God—that you have been preapproved by God and are already loved in His heart and are beautiful in His eyes?

In my senior year of high school, I (Megan) went on a camping trip to Arkansas with other student leaders from our church. In the middle of the night, our student pastor, Mark Miller, woke up the seniors and told us to get our tennis shoes on and grab a flashlight. As my best girlfriends and I stumbled sleepily out of our tents and the boys from theirs, he told us to head up a hill (more like a mountain) that was just a few yards away. We were so confused! Why were we climbing a mountain at two in the morning in total darkness? Completely out of breath, we finally reached the top of the peak. Mark led us to an area that was free of trees and shrubs and told us to lie down and look up at the sky. At this point we were exhausted but curious. When I looked up, I was in awe. I have never seen so many stars at one time. After he gave us a few minutes to relax and enjoy the scene, Mark started to talk:

> Look at the stars. Would you take any of them away? Which one doesn't belong? Did you choose one? Is one too big or too small or too bright or too dim? Even if I could, I wouldn't take one away. Why? Because if they all looked the same and were evenly spaced out across

the sky, it would be so boring! The stars are gorgeous and unique just the way they are. When you look at them all together, you can't help but stand in awe of the intricate detail and love that the Creator put into them. Well, that's exactly how God feels about us! He would never pick out one person and say, "Oh, I really messed up on that one. Why did I make her like that?" No! How stupid of us to think that. He made each of us the exact way He wanted us to be. We are the way we are for a reason, to fulfill a purpose. How boring it would be if we all looked the same, acted the same, and had the same passions and abilities. We're all designed to play our unique part in this world. The way you look, think, and act is part of God's special plan for *you*!

I dare you to go outside on a clear night and look up at the stars. Enjoy the wonder of the stars twinkling in the dark. Then look back at this page and read Mark's words to yourself as if God were saying them to you.

THE BEAUTY OF EMPTINESS

Our deep longing for love and acceptance is actually a good thing. God made us this way so we would long to be with *Him*. We're free to chase after the things of this world. But in the end it doesn't matter how many followers we have on social media, how many "likes" we get on a picture, or how many guys we have dated. It doesn't matter, because none of these things will satisfy. In the moment they may feel good, but afterward you will feel even emptier than before.

Deep down you already know this is true. You've experienced the emptiness that comes from chasing the temporary things of this world and looking in the distorted mirror of our culture. Yet you still think that if you were more popular or prettier or skinnier, had more friends, had a great boyfriend, dressed differently, and had nicer things, then maybe you would feel important. You'd be a *somebody*. Loved. Fulfilled. Beautiful.

The truth is that no matter how hard you try to complete yourself with someone or something of this world, you will never succeed. God intended this. He didn't want you to find completion and total worth anywhere but in Him. I don't say this to make you feel hopeless but to give you hope! You have been searching and trying for so long, and I am here to tell you that you can let go and give up! Stop trying. Let God take over. Let Him be your true love and the mirror you look to for your sacred reflection, the One who gives you worth and makes you feel wanted and significant. Until you realize that you will never be complete unless you find your completion in Him, you will never feel truly beautiful. I don't mean just believing God is God but actually communicating with Him and living in His truth. Let the Lord be your first and true love.

OTHER FOCUSED

Strangely enough, to become beautiful we do not start with ourselves. Beauty is much more than how we look on the outside. Real beauty is eternal and other focused. When we spend more time concentrating on other people's difficulties than on our own, we will be truly satisfied.

I've heard some suggest that before sin entered the world, Adam and Eve didn't know they were naked because they were too focused on God. When we spend our time getting to know God and becoming more like Him, we are pulled out of our selfishness. I'm not saying that all the discouraging thoughts in your head will instantly disappear and never come back. Oh, we can only dream! But I can say that those thoughts will dissipate, and you will become more joyful as your focus turns outward. You experience **JOY** when **J**esus is first, **O**thers are second, and **Y**ou are third.

We all have hidden hurts. Right now you might feel like running away and licking your wounds. That would be comforting, right? Wrong. Don't sit there and dwell in a tub of loneliness. Go help others out of *their* misery. When you reach out to someone else, not only do you give that person hope and love, but you receive it too.

What do you do when your car's gas tank is empty? You find a gas station and fill it up. But imagine that you live on a planet without gas stations. Instead every car is equipped with a simple siphoning device that makes it easy to share fuel, and each car's gas tank is magically refilled with twice the amount that is given away.

What will you do on this imaginary planet when your car runs low on gas? Let's say you have a quarter tank of gas. The wisest thing would be to find someone who needs a quarter tank of gas and give yours away. Now you have a half tank. Find someone who can use a half tank, and your own gas gauge reads "Full" again.

On this planet you'd naturally be on the lookout for people who could use some extra gas. You'd always be aware that you needed to give away what you had.

Here's a hard fact: in this moment in your community, there are people with heavier burdens than your own, people who just need to be loved. Do you remember that overwhelming feeling of satisfaction and joy you get from helping someone? The happiness you feel that's totally out of proportion with the tiny kindness you gave? Is your emotional tank empty? The best way to become joyful is to pour yourself into someone else. Do you need encouragement? Find someone to encourage. Are you running on fumes? Go help someone else. There is always somebody to love.

Whenever I (Megan) was having a bad day in college, I would call my mom, hoping for some words of encouragement and for her to say she felt sorry for me and wished she could help. When you are having a bad day, sometimes you want to be pitied. It feels good when the focus is on you and people are aware you are struggling. But instead, she usually responded by saying, "I'm so sorry you are having a hard time. You should go help someone else who is having a worse day than you." Those were never the words I wanted to hear. Why would I want to help someone else when I was feeling down? I never felt like following her advice, but I was always glad when I did. It really put life in perspective.

When I helped someone who was hurting, good came from it every single time. Not only would the other person be encouraged, but I would leave filled with joy and be uplifted myself. It is simply amazing how God fills our tanks when we fill someone else's. When all of life seems like a struggle and you feel as if you're slogging through wet cement, remind yourself that someone else is having a worse day than you and that God can use you to bring joy to both of you.

Reflection

1. I want to challenge you. Instead of taking another selfie and posting it, how about taking a picture of someone else instead? Consider taking a picture of someone you know who radiates true beauty and writing a short caption of what makes that person beautiful to you. Begin the habit of taking the focus off yourself and putting it on others.

2. Read and meditate on the mirror of truth in this verse: "You are altogether beautiful, my darling; there is no flaw in you" (Song of Solomon 4:7), and remember that God says these words to you.

Prayer

Lord, not many days go by without my comparing myself to another woman. I know, I know, that's such a dead end. Open my eyes to see the beauty of Your plan in creating each of us to be different. And open my heart to the needs of others, to those places where I can reach out and touch other people's lives with Your grace and truth. Amen.

Fancy hairstyles **don't** make you beautiful. Wearing gold jewelry or fine clothes **doesn't** make you beautiful. Instead, your **beauty** comes from **inside you.** It is the beauty of a **gentle** and **quiet spirit.** Beauty like this **doesn't fade away.** God places **great value** on it.

1 PETER 3:3–4, NIrV

The Beautiful Struggle

He will give a crown of beauty for ashes,
a joyous blessing instead of mourning.

—ISAIAH 61:3, NLT

God always ignores the present perfection for
the ultimate perfection.

—OSWALD CHAMBERS

4

The Beauty of Brokenness

Beauty Begins in Total Surrender

We rejoice in our sufferings, knowing that suffering produces endurance, and endurance produces character, and character produces hope.

—ROMANS 5:3–4, ESV

Every where the greater joy is ushered in by the greater pain.

—SAINT AUGUSTINE

t is never easy to deal with depression or any event or situation
that makes you feel an overwhelming amount of despair and
loneliness. I (Megan) have experienced those feelings of utter
desolation and hopelessness, believing there was no point to life,
no reason for living, and having no feelings but sadness and
worthlessness. I have been in the worst place imaginable. All I
wanted to do was sit in my room and cry or, better, just sleep for
hours since it was the closest thing to not being alive.

In high school I was known as a very happy and energetic
girl. People would ask me if I ever stopped smiling. I loved
being funny and cheering people up. Honestly, it was difficult

for me not to smile and be happy. It's who God had made me to be. I wondered how people could want to hurt or kill themselves. It didn't make sense to me. There is always something to live for, and I could not fathom the possibility of being so low and defeated that I felt like dying or taking my own life.

I couldn't understand until I felt that way myself. My freshman year of college I was hit with an uncontrollable wave of despair. I found myself believing there was no meaning to life and being so sad and upset and in such pain that I felt nothing would make me happier than to go on to heaven. In a way I was right. We are meant for heaven, and nothing on this earth is going to totally satisfy us. But we are also meant to live satisfying and fulfilling lives while here on earth!

People had told me that college would be the best four years of my life. Though some of my best memories come from my college days, I can also say that those four years were the most difficult of my life. I had absolutely loved high school. I was a cheerleader, had amazing friends, made good grades, was involved at church, and had everything going for me—except I wasn't very close to the Lord.

That first year of college I had only a couple of friends. I wasn't involved in anything. My family was three hours away. I didn't know how to study. I was discouraged and terribly lonely. These factors, along with a genetic tendency, combined to create the perfect storm of clinical depression.

NO PLACE TO LOOK BUT UP

In a big way I'm grateful I've had to deal with depression, because it has taught me to depend on God! And being the selfish person I am, I needed that. I needed God to kick the pedestal out from under me so I would realize that life isn't all about me and that I actually do need Him. During the most difficult time, I would wake up every morning with my eyes wide open to God and say, "Lord, I definitely cannot get through this day without You. Please help me follow You today, and bring me joy through this difficult time." I *had* to read my Bible every day. I *had* to pray continually. I *had* to grow closer to God. Man, I hated the loneliness and pain. But, wow, did I love growing closer to God! I grew so close to God through that time. Life began to have meaning and importance again, and I started to find joy in the little things. I finally turned my attention from myself to God and started letting Him love other people through me.

God has taken my depression and used it—more than anything else in my life—to deepen my faith. That's the beauty of brokenness. God has used my pain and problems to bring me to the end of myself so I would depend totally on Him. He has also taught me that I need to humbly accept the help of others, including a Christian doctor whom God has used greatly in my continued healing. Beauty begins where self-reliance ends.

Think about it. If everything were perfect in your life, you wouldn't need God. You wouldn't pray and connect with Him. You wouldn't rely on Him. And you would miss out on the whole reason you were created—to be in a relationship with your Creator.

My brokenness leads me to the Beautiful One and the true source of my beauty. Beauty begins in brokenness, because beauty begins when I come to the end of myself and totally surrender to Him.

Some of you are going through a painful season in your life, and it certainly doesn't feel beautiful. Just know that God has the power to take the shattered pieces of our lives and make something beautiful out of them. Everyone has had a broken heart, and some of you are facing broken hearts right now. Some of you have just gone through the pain of divorce, and your hearts have been crushed. Some of you have lost a loved one, and your hearts are aching. Some of you have a child who is living in rebellion, and your hearts have been decimated. Every moment of every day your heart gets ripped apart. Just know this: there is a God who holds your heart together. He will heal your heart. He's the only One who can. Psalm 34:18 says, "The LORD is close to the brokenhearted and saves those who are crushed in spirit."

If you have a broken heart today, God has never been closer than He is right now. He's right next to you. He is right there to bring healing. Surrender your broken heart to Him so He can make something beautiful out of it. Let Him begin healing your heart. He wants you to know how incredibly precious you are to Him.

THE MIRACLE IS IN THE MESS

I used to think of miracles as being like a knight appearing in shining armor on a white horse or a fairy godmother swooping her wand. Poof! Everything's perfect. The truth is that life is messy, and God works best in the midst of that mess. Life is a beautiful mess most of the time. It's beautiful because God gets into the mess with us and turns it into a miracle.

Yes, I was having a hard time, but to think that others were struggling too and maybe didn't have family, friends, or God to comfort them was very humbling. Not having anyone who cared? That would be a harder situation than mine. So I tried to do what my mom said. It was hard at times to stop thinking about how sad I was and to focus on other people. But it was so worth it. Turning my attention to other people not only took my mind off my current situation, but it also brought me joy in that difficult time. When I thought it was impossible for me to feel happy or any loving emotion, I found that is just what happened.

I began to see God working a miracle in the middle of my

mess. Did my depression completely go away? No, but during that difficult time I finally had hope that God was going to bring me out of it. Repeatedly I would forget and feel as if the sadness would never end, but whenever I took my eyes off myself and put them on God and others, I felt hopeful and okay. Sometimes it was just the little acts of kindness that brought me satisfaction.

During my most difficult semester, I had a lot of time to myself in my apartment when my three roommates were in class. I decided not to sit idly in my room but to do something. I would make my roommates' beds, tidy up their rooms, clean and fold their laundry, and leave them encouraging, loving notes on their desks. My motive wasn't to get attention from them. I just knew they would feel better coming home to a welcoming room after a stressful day of school. Seeing and knowing their joy brought me joy. While I was busy filling their cups, God was filling mine. Helping others brings us joy on normal days, and in the hard times this overwhelming feeling of fulfillment and joy can be enough to break us free from our chains of despair and loneliness.

Let me (Chris) give a word of encouragement to all of you who are moms. I hate to break it to you, but in the messiness of life, you're going to make mistakes. There will be times when you blow it. There will be times when you try really hard to do the right thing for your kids, but what you do will turn out to be the wrong thing. I've found, however, that my kids are remarkably forgiving when I come to them and say, "I blew it. I'm sorry. I was really trying. It was not my intent to make such a mess, but I did. I was wrong. Please forgive me." Then we talk about how things could be different next time.

You have a lot of influence in your child's life, and the way to keep that influence is by asking for forgiveness when you make mistakes, even though you had good intentions. Avoiding that honesty will cause you to lose influence with your kids. You may end up talking, but no one will be listening. When you abandon the responsibility to engage in their lives and get in their messes with them, you lose credibility. Our lives are messy. Our kids' lives are messy too, and it takes an incredible amount of intentionality to stay engaged with them.

But if you'll hold on even when it's tough—especially when it's tough—when you're both hurting, when you don't know what to do, then you will always have an influence on your child's life. Stay in the game. Don't give up and don't let go. If the steering wheel slips for a minute, grab it and pull it back. Fully engage. Get involved in the mess of their lives with them. Remember that God sees and knows the details, and He is big enough, has grace enough, and loves you and your child enough that He is going to see you both through. He's going to see you to the other side.

By the way, just because you messed up in the past, never

believe the lie that your mistake has disqualified you from ever speaking about that issue with your child. When you talk to your kids about drinking, relationship issues, sex, or any of the myriad other things they face, don't let Satan's lies keep you from guiding them with the truth. Many well-intentioned parents tell me, "Well, to be honest, I did the same things when I was their age, so I'd be a hypocrite if I said, 'Don't do that.'" They feel they've been disqualified from speaking about that issue. Nothing could be further from the truth.

If you were leading your daughter down a hiking trail and halfway down the path you suddenly fell into a ditch covered with poison ivy and filled with snakes, wouldn't you warn her? Wouldn't you yell, "Stop! Don't take another step! This is a bad path!" Of course you'd warn her! So why do we hesitate to warn our children about real-life ditches we've fallen into? The Enemy uses a strange mixture of pride and the fear of hypocrisy to silence us in the very areas where our kids need us the most. Far from being disqualified, you're actually in a *great* position to talk to your kids if you've made the same mistake in the past. You can help them avoid the hurt that you had to endure. The mistakes you've made give you the authority to say, "You know what? I've been down that road, and let me tell you, it's awful. I still have scars from it. I love you, and I don't want to see you go through the same thing."

It takes a lot of courage to stop hiding behind the mistakes in the past. Just know that if you chicken out and remain silent, it's like removing the stop sign from a busy intersection. So speak up! Say, "Don't go this way," and then try to help your children find a different path. Let them learn from the mistakes you've made. We think we need to clean up our mess before God can work a miracle, but the opposite is true. God is waiting for us to invite Him into our mess because He's the only One who can clean it up. He takes our messes and turns them into miracles.

YOUR MESS IS YOUR MESSAGE

Many times I have asked God why He has allowed me (Megan) to experience depression. Only after I was able to walk with another girl through her depression did I finally realize that beauty could come from such an ugly thing. Scripture tells us, "He comes alongside us when we go through hard times, and before you know it, he brings us alongside someone else who is going through hard times so that we can be there for that person just as God was there for us" (2 Corinthians 1:4, MSG).

God has taken my biggest mess and turned it into my most powerful message! God is turning the ashes of my depression into the beauty of His purpose. He has a way of taking our brokenness and making something beautiful out of it. The most beautiful people I've ever known are those who experienced great pain and loss but moved deeper into God's love instead of becoming bitter. You can see the beauty of Christ reflected in their compassion for others.

I think one reason we're drawn to the beauty of brokenness is because we can all relate. You impress people when you talk about your strengths, but you influence people when you admit your struggles. I'm drawn to people who are honest about their struggles and pain. Don't hide your messes. Admit them to God and invite Him to start working a miracle in your life. Then be transparent with others so they can see the beauty of Christ reflected through your brokenness. One of my favorite scriptures is 2 Corinthians 4:7:

> But we have this treasure in jars of clay to show that this
> all-surpassing power is from God and not from us.

We are jars of clay on the outside, but on the inside we carry the beauty and brilliance of Christ. The more cracked and broken the jar of clay is, the more Christ's power and beauty shine through. Don't try to hide your brokenness. If you do, you'll become bitter. There is nothing more ugly and devastating than bitterness.

Bring the broken pieces of your life to God, and let Him make something beautiful out of them. Ask Him to take the mess of your mistakes, sins, and failures and turn them into His miracle. Let Him take the ashes of your greatest pain and brokenness and turn them into a brilliant and beautiful light that brings beauty to others.

Reflection

1. Read this passage from Isaiah 61:3 (NLT): "He will give a crown of beauty for ashes, a joyous blessing instead of mourning." Put it on your mirror to remind you that God reflects His beauty in the broken places of your life.

2. Ask God to help you get your focus off yourself and on the needs of others. Think of one small way you could bring beauty into someone else's life, and then do it. It might be watching a single mom's young children while she does errands, raking the yard of an elderly neighbor, or asking a lonely friend to join you for lunch.

Prayer

Lord, some days just feel too much for me, or I blow it with a close friend or family member. Some days I'm just a mess. You know that. Help me as I continue to learn that You don't turn away from me on those dark days, but You are actually close to my broken heart. Thank You for the miracles You create out of my messy days. You truly are beautiful, O God! Amen.

We **rejoice** in our sufferings, knowing that suffering produces **endurance**, and endurance produces **character**, and character produces **hope**.

Romans 5:3–4, ESV

5

The Daily Battle

Beauty Begins, but the Struggle Doesn't End

This is what the LORD says to you: "Do not
be afraid or discouraged because of this vast
army. For the battle is not yours, but God's."

—2 CHRONICLES 20:15

Relying on God has to begin all over again
every day as if nothing had yet been done.

—C. S. LEWIS

Today you have a life-altering decision to make. You get to choose whether to look in the distorted mirrors of self, parents, peers, spouses, or boyfriends *or* to look in the mirror of God's truth. Which are you going to choose today? Choosing to see your sacred reflection in God's eyes is a daily decision and, therefore, a lifelong battle! I would love it if I decided one day to stop looking at myself through the distorted mirror of our culture and then for the rest of my life I lived from my true beauty. But that would be too easy, and as we all know, this world isn't easy. We have to intentionally make the decision every day to see ourselves through the eyes of God's truth. We have to choose to see the beautiful women He created us to be and choose to stop putting ourselves down and listening to Satan's lies.

We are going to struggle every single day with this choice, and that's okay, because it reminds us that we need to depend on God. The struggle itself has a beauty, because it makes our faith grow stronger, and our character becomes more like Christ's and, therefore, more beautiful. Every time we choose to focus on the mirror of Christ's truth instead of Satan's lies, our faith is strengthened.

I'm madly in love with my husband, but that doesn't mean I naturally act lovingly toward him every day. That doesn't mean I never get upset with him or feel like being selfish. Love is not merely a feeling. It is also a decision. Even if I don't *feel* like loving him at the moment for whatever reason, I still have to choose to *act* in a loving way. Maintaining the proper self-image works the same way. It requires discipline. We don't always feel like reading our Bible or even getting out of bed. But we have to choose to do so anyway.

We have to push past our selfish, earthly desires and strive toward the true desires of our hearts. In our brokenness our natural instinct is to be selfish. But if Christ is in our lives, we have new desires. We have to push past those fleshly wants to discover what we truly long for.

THE THORN OF INSECURITY

A man in the Bible named Paul was given "a thorn" in his flesh, something he constantly struggled with that kept him from becoming proud and required him to lean on the Lord's power and not his own.

> If I wanted to boast, I would be no fool in doing so, because I would be telling the truth. But I won't do it, because I don't want anyone to give me credit beyond what they can see in my life or hear in my message, even though I have received such wonderful revelations from God. So to keep me from becoming proud, I was given a thorn in my flesh, a messenger from Satan to torment me and keep me from becoming proud. Three different times I begged the Lord to take it away. Each time he said, "My grace is all you need. My power works best in weakness." So now I am glad to boast about my weaknesses, so that the power of Christ can work through me. That's why I take pleasure in my weaknesses, and in the insults, hardships, persecutions, and troubles that I suffer for Christ. For when I am weak, then I am strong. (2 Corinthians 12:6–10, NLT)

I believe, as a woman, that one of our biggest thorns is this constant insecurity about our looks, our personalities, our bodies, our talents—who we are. This thorn reminds me of Paul's thorn. Paul prayed for God to take it away, but instead God said, "I'll give you the grace to overcome, and I'll use your thorn to demonstrate My power through you." This thorn of insecurity will probably be something we battle for the rest of our lives, but God says to us the same thing He said to Paul, "I'll give you the grace to overcome, and I'll use your thorn to demonstrate My power through you."

We think the thorn is our looks or our bodies, so we focus on changing our appearance. But the thorn we need to fight against is our mind-set. We try to fix "problems" with the way we look, when the real problem is the way we think. We're trying to fix our bodies, when we need to be looking to Jesus so He can fix our mind-set.

Yes, it's a daily battle to choose the mirror of God's truth over the mirror of Satan's lies. Yes, it's a daily, moment-by-moment struggle to live in the truth that we are beautiful. But I want to say a resounding *yes* to the fact that there is victory in the struggle! The victory comes when we let our insecurities push us deeper into the secure arms of God.

But here's something important: you have to stop beating yourself up when you lose one of these daily battles, because

Christ has already won the war. Because of what Christ did on the cross, we now have complete forgiveness for all our failures.

When you mess up and choose to believe Satan's lie that you're not beautiful, he hits you with a second lie. Satan whispers, "God doesn't love you because you keep losing the battle. You're such a loser!"

Nothing could be further from the truth! When you lose a battle, the loss doesn't make you a loser. When you fail, that doesn't make you a failure. God's love for you doesn't wane when you sin and disobey Him. You don't change the truth of your true beauty when you make an ugly mess of things. Your beauty comes from God, and it's eternal. God's love for you never changes. You have to choose to rest in His love.

The problem is not the struggle to feel beautiful. The problem is that we don't turn to God in the struggle. In the book *One Month to Live,* I (Chris) wrote this:

> When my son Josh was four or five years old, I took him to the park one day, and he immediately ran to his favorite spot. "Hold me up on the monkey bars," he said. So I lifted him up, and he grabbed the monkey bars, and I let go. His little shoes hung about five feet off the ground, and he was so proud, holding on all

by himself with a huge smile on his face. After about a minute he got tired and said, "Okay, get me down."

I said, "Josh, just let go, and I'll catch you."

He got a worried look on his face and said, "No, get me down."

I said, "Well, Josh, if you just let go, I'll catch you."

"No, get me down."

"Josh, I love you. I promise, I'll catch you."[11]

Some of you may be wondering what kind of parent I am! Others may realize I was taking the opportunity for a teaching moment so Josh would know that he could trust me, that if he'd just let go, I'd be there for him. But that little guy held on with all his might until his knuckles turned white and he couldn't hold on any longer. Finally he let go, and I caught him.

A big smile came across his face, and I set him down, and he ran off to play on the swings. He forgot all about it. But it struck me that God had a message for me in this scene, almost as if He were saying, "This is exactly the way you relate to Me. You hold on desperately, trying to do things in your own strength. You struggle endlessly, trying to make everything just right, trying to please people, trying to control every situation. You hold on and think there's no one to catch you so you'd better grip harder and cling tighter. While you're hanging there and your knuckles are turning white, I'm saying, 'Just let go, and I'll catch you. Just let go. I promise you that I love you and I'll catch you.'"

When you're in the middle of the daily struggles, I encourage you to let go and let God catch you. Let God's loving, strong arms hold you. Then rest in His love and in the truth of your sacred reflection in His eyes. Just listen to Jesus's words in Matthew 11:28–30 (MSG).

> Are you tired? Worn out? Burned out on religion? Come to me. Get away with me and you'll recover your life. I'll show you how to take a real rest. Walk with me and work with me—watch how I do it. Learn the unforced rhythms of grace. I won't lay anything heavy or ill-fitting on you. Keep company with me and you'll learn to live freely and lightly.

There don't appear to be any prerequisites here other than being tired and worn out. If that describes you, then you have a decision to make. Will you spend your one-and-only life trying to change your body and chasing after acceptance, the approval of others, popularity, and attention, or will you rest in the love and approval of Christ? We are all given the choice. What will you choose today?

THE TENSION OF BEAUTY

There will always be tension between your flesh and your spirit. For most decisions in your life, your flesh will tell you to do one thing, and your spirit will tell you to do the opposite. It is easy to give in to the flesh, but only the Spirit will reward you in the end.

You will never be satisfied if you keep running after earthly things. You can have everything you need, but if you can't be thankful or see God through it all and notice Him in everything, then you will never be content. And you'll never feel truly beautiful until you find your sacred reflection in Christ's eyes. Solomon, king of Jerusalem, wrote in Ecclesiastes 2 about all the things he accomplished on this earth and how he gave in to his fleshly desires. In the middle of the chapter, he said,

> I denied myself nothing my eyes desired;
> > I refused my heart no pleasure.
> My heart took delight in all my labor,
> > and this was the reward for all my toil.
> Yet when I surveyed all that my hands had done
> > and what I had toiled to achieve,
> everything was meaningless, a chasing after the wind;
> > nothing was gained under the sun. (verses 10–11)

Solomon concluded that everything is meaningless unless we focus on the things that are eternal. And remember, true beauty is eternal, but pretty is only temporary. All the hours I spend on myself in front of the mirror trying to look pretty have no value for eternity. It's wasted time. But the time I spend reflecting the beauty and love of Christ to others will make a lasting difference for eternity.

The question is, are you going to spend most of your time on things that won't last, like being popular, partying, and changing your body? Or will you spend most of your time on things that will last forever? The only things that matter and are eternal are loving God and loving others. Jesus said:

> "Love the Lord your God with all your heart and with all your soul and with all your mind." This is the first and greatest commandment. And the second is like it: "Love your neighbor as yourself." All the Law and the Prophets hang on these two commandments. (Matthew 22:37–40)

Love the Lord your God, and love your neighbor. This is our purpose and calling on this earth. How simple! We're to look in the mirror of Christ to see our sacred reflections, and then we're to reflect Christ's love to others. These two things are what we need to base our lives on. This is why we are alive. Don't get caught up in the meaningless things of this world. Remember the big picture. Don't spend years wasting your time and then look back and ask yourself, *What did I do to make a difference?* If you know the goal in life is to love God and love others, don't let yourself get distracted and waste time on earthly things that bring only temporary satisfaction. We all forget sometimes, and we let ourselves get caught up in pointless things, but don't let the past ruin the way you live your future. Let it drive you that much more toward what is eternal. Do you want your life to have meaning? Then start doing something meaningful!

LOSE YOUR BURDENS AND WIN THE BATTLE

I absolutely hate seeing girls and women struggle with eating disorders and their self-image. It hurts my heart so much sometimes that I want to take on their burden so they don't have to deal with it. I try to explain how beautiful they are and how they deserve so much more, but some never understand. I can't show them how much they are worth because it doesn't matter how much they are worth to me; it only matters how much they are worth to God. I want them to realize that God loves them more than I ever could.

God loves us so much that He gave His life so we wouldn't

have to carry the weight of guilt and shame. We don't have to take on this burden! Is that not a relief? Doesn't it make you want to jump for joy? Let me say that again. Our God—not a mere human—but our God *died* for *us*. He died for our freedom. He died for us, so we shouldn't put ourselves down. He died so we could have a glimpse of His unconditional love for us.

He thinks you're so valuable that you're worth dying for. He was tortured and ridiculed, and He experienced the most excruciating kind of death so you might follow Him. It wasn't even a sure thing, but the mere possibility, that you would decide one day to follow Him and accept the love He holds out to you. Picture a father dying a horrible death for his unborn daughter so she could live, while knowing that his daughter might one day choose to turn against the values he held dear. That's what God did for you and me! To Him, we were worth the chance. Even if you were the only person on earth, He still would have died for you because He believes you are worth dying for.

> You see, at just the right time, when we were still
> powerless, Christ died for the ungodly. Very rarely will
> anyone die for a righteous person, though for a good
> person someone might possibly dare to die. But God
> demonstrates his own love for us in this: While we were
> still sinners, Christ died for us. (Romans 5:6–8)

With friends and boyfriends at times you may have to rewin their affection. With some people you have to work to earn their approval and maintain their acceptance. But that's not the way it is with God. Your acceptance and value were settled at the Cross! God gave His unconditional love and acceptance when He took your sins upon Himself.

The only way to win this battle to feel beautiful is to lose the burden of striving to feel accepted. We have a God who is big enough and strong enough to carry all our burdens and problems, especially the *big burden*—the need to feel total acceptance and love. Every moment of every day I must choose to roll that heavy burden onto God. If I don't give the burden to Him, the weight of it will crush the life out of me. But when I consciously choose to roll the burden onto the Lord, I feel as light as a feather, freed from the oppressive need to win others' approval.

Yes, I still struggle, and at times I hold on to the burden and lose my battle to feel beautiful. There are still so many things I want to change about myself, even as I write this book, but as I am writing this, I am also hitting myself on the head because I desperately need this reminder! Thank goodness you and I have a Father who loves us just the way we are. A Father who loves us when we disobey. A Father who loves us when we don't love ourselves and the bodies He made. A Father whose heart hurts when our hearts hurt. A Father who will never leave us or let us go and is with us every step of the way. A Father who gave His life for us selfish, sinful, and sometimes foolish girls who just want to be loved. And in return He receives just the drops of love we give Him here and there, compared to the massive oceans of love He pours upon us.

Oh, how undeserving we are, and how great is our God. The least we can do for Him is appreciate, take care of, and love the person, personality, and body He handcrafted for us.

YOU ARE PRICELESS

The first time my husband and I (Chris) went to the Louvre in Paris, we headed straight for Leonardo da Vinci's sixteenth-century oil painting of the woman with the enigmatic smile. I have to be honest. When I first saw the *Mona Lisa,* I thought, *What's the big deal?* The painting wasn't what I expected. First, it is small. It's only thirty inches by twenty-one inches. You have to understand that the Louvre houses all these stunning works of art that are so colorful and cover whole walls. And then there is the *Mona Lisa* in this small frame.

Second, the woman in the painting is just as plain and ordinary and unexciting as she is in all the reproductions I've seen on television and in movies through the years. I thought, *How could something that at first glance seems so plain and ordinary and unexciting be so great?* Well, I just revealed how little I know about art because the *Mona Lisa* is the most valuable master-piece in the world. It is owned by the French government, and it's uninsured because it's priceless. No one can put a price tag on the most famous painting in Western art history.

At first glance my untrained eye didn't see the value of the *Mona Lisa*. Maybe you feel as though no one sees your value and worth, and maybe even you have a hard time seeing your true worth. Perhaps it seems all the things you do are small and insignificant, mundane, ordinary, and plain. But God says you are a work of art! You are a priceless work of art. In fact, no one can put a price tag on how valuable you are!

> For we are God's masterpiece. He has created us
> anew in Christ Jesus, so we can do the good things
> he planned for us long ago. (Ephesians 2:10, NLT)

We have to choose to agree with God that we are priceless—utter masterpieces. It is a fact that we are beautiful and priceless. We just have to choose to believe this truth.

> Look at the birds of the air; they do not sow or reap or
> store away in barns, and yet your heavenly Father feeds
> them. Are you not much more valuable than they?
> (Matthew 6:26)

God takes care of the birds and the flowers, yet they are nothing compared to how much you are worth to Him. So if He takes care of these things that mean nothing, how much more do you think He will take care of His daughters?

Even though you know you are worth more than all the gold in the world, you may still struggle with your thorn of feeling insecure. Whenever you feel down and worthless, just remember that these lies are coming from the devil. He will do whatever he can to bring you down, especially if you are bringing others to Christ. Satan has really been on my tail as I have written this book. I have felt that I am not beautiful and that I need to work out more and eat less and change my body, and I have been craving the attention of others. Why is this happening? Because I am trying to get the truth out to the world.

When I remember that the devil goes after those who follow God, it encourages me even more to keep going. I want to show the devil that he cannot stop me. If he is taking the time to try to ruin my life, he must know that I am about to do something great! So let this encourage you. The devil doesn't go after people who are already living in sin or aren't doing anything with the good knowledge they have. He goes after people who are making a difference. So when you feel down and defeated, remind yourself that you must be doing something right. Then let that knowledge excite you and inspire you to keep doing what you are doing.

You will mess up, you will sin, and at times you will forget this truth and believe the Enemy's lies. Don't beat yourself up when this happens. All of us are imperfect and will mess up again. But don't let this slip-up keep you from pressing toward the goal. Don't get caught up in the idea that you sinned and wallow in that. Ask for forgiveness from God, and move on! Satan draws you into sin by making you feel the sin is okay. Then once you sin, he makes you feel horrible for doing it. You will still sin at times, but you don't have to stay in that feeling of worthlessness.

A REAL RELATIONSHIP

In my later years in high school, I (Megan) figured out what it meant to talk to God. I first asked Christ into my heart when I was a little girl. I prayed, read my Bible, and truly believed in Him and tried to live my life for Him. But it wasn't until my junior year of high school, when I was in a Bible study led by my student pastor, Mark Miller, that I truly experienced a real relationship with God. I always thought I had a relationship with Him, but as I think about it in retrospect, I really didn't. I believed in Him, but having a relationship is different from just believing He exists. I have a strong relationship with my parents, brothers, friends, and husband. I talk with them almost every day and not just at a surface level. They know my deepest struggles, my favorite things, what makes me happy, what makes me sad, my annoying habits, my successes, and my sins, and yet they love me so much! These are real relationships!

What if we treated God the way we treat our boyfriends or husbands—talking to Him throughout the day, and when we weren't talking to Him, we were thinking about Him? I realized I didn't have that with God but desperately wanted it. No one had told me that I could just talk to Him out loud like a friend! That's just crazy! So I tried it. My favorite place to talk to God is in my car. Sometimes I even buckle the passenger seat belt to acknowledge His presence, and then I just talk. I tell Him about my day—how frustrated I am with a situation or a person, how happy and excited I am about something, and how difficult some circumstances are for me. I am honest, real, and open just as I am with a best friend or my spouse. Yes, He already knows what I'm going through and what I'm thinking, but this truly draws me closer to Him. He wants to hear my heart in my own words. When we pray, God already knows what we are going to say, but we do it anyway because we believe in Him and we need to talk to Him. How do you grow closer to your friends? You spend time with them.

STICKY-NOTE TRUTH

I love to write verses on sticky notes and place them around the house. What is more practical and encouraging than reading a verse when you are brushing your teeth or getting food from the fridge? When I was in college and living in an apartment, I put sticky notes on my mirrors and even wrote on the mirrors in Expo markers. They'd say things like "Don't worry. Pray!" Or "Rely on God, not your own strength." Or "Who can I bless today?"

I even had a sticky note on my steering wheel when I was in high school. It eventually faded from the sunlight, but every day I was reminded of that bit of wisdom on the steering wheel. And I wrote other verses and encouragements on sticky notes when I came across something that stood out to me. The idea is to put these small notes of love and encouragement in high-traffic areas—places where you will see them frequently during your day. After a while I would get used to the verses I saw so often and would look at them but not actually read them or take them in. When this happened, I replaced them with new verses.

As we said, fighting Satan's lies will not be easy, but it is very possible. As long as you stay constantly connected to God, you can do this. You can overcome the tormenting thoughts of the devil. You can feel satisfied with yourself and who God made you to be. You are absolutely beautiful. Choose to believe it today.

Reflection

1. Here's a challenge. Take a sticky note and write on it "Thank You for making me beautiful." Stick it on the mirror you use most. It's okay if you're not sure you believe it yet. My hope is that very soon you will.

2. What is the heaviest burden you're carrying right now? Personalize Philippians 4:13 as a prayer, and specifically name that burden. For example, *I can reject body shaming through You, O Lord, who gives me strength.* Then ask God to take the weight of the problem off your shoulders and carry you as well. Thank Him that He's strong enough to carry your burdens and hold you.

Prayer

Please take the weight of the tough situation I'm facing off me, O Lord, and remind me that You are my strength. I am so tired of trying to carry this burden day after day. I believe You are strong enough to carry it and kind enough to keep me close to You at the same time. Thank You for hearing me when I pray. Amen.

Three different times I begged the Lord to take it away. Each time he said, "**My grace** is all you need. **My power** works best in weakness." So now I am glad to boast about my weaknesses, so that the **power of Christ** can work through me.... For when I am weak, then **I am strong**.

2 CORINTHIANS 12:8–10, NLT

6

A Beautiful Team

Beauty Begins with the Right Friends

There are "friends" who destroy each other,
but a real friend sticks closer than a brother.

—PROVERBS 18:24, NLT

For beautiful eyes, look for the good in others;
for beautiful lips, speak only words of kindness; and for poise, walk with the knowledge
that you are never alone.

—AUDREY HEPBURN

Over the years we have talked with many girls and women who struggle with choosing their relationships. They have finally realized that their friends or boyfriends do not treat them well, which is an accomplishment in itself, but they feel as if they are trapped and have no alternative but to stay in a relationship with these people. The truth is, people *do* have a choice! Crazy, I know, but we actually get to choose our friends! I don't mean to lessen the difficulty of choosing good friends, but we should wake up to the power that we most definitely have.

In this struggle to live from our sacred reflections and reflect Christ's beauty to others, we must surround ourselves with "beautiful" friends—friends who will stand in the struggle with us and build us up in the battle. We have to choose our friends wisely because we will become like the people we hang around. When I (Megan) started my freshman year at college, I had no friends there. I knew who my roommate was, and I had a couple of acquaintances from high school, but I had no true, close friends. It was awful. I absolutely hated it. I met some cool people my first semester, but before I knew it, everyone around me seemed to have found their lifelong friends. I felt totally out of the loop, as if I was never going to find a close group of friends. One truth I felt the Lord telling me through this time was to be patient and not rush into relationships with people just because I felt lonely and unwanted. I felt Him telling me that if I would just wait, He would bring the right people into my life at the right time. So that's what I did. Was it easy? Not at all. I hated it actually. But was it worth it? More than anything! It was worth being lonely and sad for a semester to receive those beautiful friends.

If you are a student changing schools or going off to college, hold out for those beautiful friends. If you are an adult moving to a new city for a job or family, the same applies. Don't rush into the first group you find just because you feel awkward and want to be affirmed by others. Hold out for that God-selected group of women who are going to encourage and uplift you.

FRIEND OR FOE

This may sound weird, but let's evaluate our friendships. Here are some questions to ask:

- Do your friends make you feel loved and important?
- Do they encourage you?
- Do they put you down?
- Do they pressure you into things?
- Do they talk about you behind your back?
- Do they stick with you in the hard times?
- Are they involved in church, and do they have a relationship with God?
- Is being popular important to them?
- Are they involved in partying, drugs, or sex outside of marriage?

As you go through these questions, you might be thinking that you fit some of these descriptions of poor friends. Don't get too consumed with the idea that you might be bringing others down, but realize it and choose to change. Also, if you and your group of friends are having trouble, this can be an opportunity for all of you to band together and decide to change as a group. But the most difficult situation is when you confront your friends about their actions and, sadly, they choose to stick with the way they are living, at the expense of your friendship. However, sometimes it comes down to that, and you have to make the difficult decision to lose a friendship in order to gain or retain a beautiful character.

Asking yourself these questions can help you see if your relationships with your friends need to change. You don't have a choice of parents or family, but you can choose your friends. This might be the right time for you to make a bold choice and change your relationships. I hope that by reading this section you realize what God is asking you to do—whether that is moving on from your friends and finding a whole new group, or leading your friends toward God. If you are struggling to know the right thing to do, then spend some time with God, and ask Him for direction. When we spend time with God by reading the Bible, praying, and talking to Him, we become more like Him, and He will guide us every step of the way.

TOO MANY FISH IN THE SEA

I (Megan) think the only reason we should date is to find our husbands. But this usually isn't our reason for being with a guy. Most of the time it is because a guy shows interest in us, which we feel hardly ever happens, so we jump into the relationship. And it helps if he's nice and good looking too. What more does a girl need? But why do we do this? We know we aren't going to marry this guy. But we think he is going to somehow fill that void in us, that desire to be wanted and loved. We think, *Finally, somebody likes me!*

I know that feeling all too well. It was the main reason I dated in high school. An attractive, godly, funny guy showed interest in me, and I jumped into a dating relationship with him. Ladies, hold out for that truly awesome guy who fits only you. There are plenty of amazing guys in this world, but I believe only *one* of them has been prepared and set aside for you by God. It isn't bad to date. I honestly think dating makes a lot of sense if you are doing it for the right reasons. What I am saying is that we don't need to jump from guy to guy in order to feel good about ourselves. In the end that will leave us empty because we give a piece of our heart to each guy we grow close to.

If you have a boyfriend, this is the time to evaluate your relationship with him. Here are some questions to ask yourself:

- Does he have a relationship with God and attend church regularly?
- Does he treat me like a princess?
- Does he pressure me into sexual acts?
- Does he respect me, my parents, and my friends?
- Does he treasure our time together?

- Are his friends involved in the right things?
- Does he pull me away from my friends?
- Does he believe in waiting until marriage to have sex?

There are many more questions I could add, but these are a good start and will help you know if the guy you are dating is worth your time and effort. If your boyfriend failed in one of these areas, please don't think I am telling you to break up with him right away. But also, please do not overlook it. I am hoping these questions will give you an idea of how your boyfriend is treating you and if he has the qualities you want in a husband, which should be the reason you are dating him in the first place.

WHERE DO YOU LOOK?

Where do you look for affirmation and love? The number of "likes" you get on your Instagram post? How much attention you get from guys when you wear that skimpy outfit? Maybe you look for it from your kids or your husband. It is easy to get caught up in the things of this world. God has called us to live in the world but not be of it. So many things are available to us that distract us from God. I am guilty of getting caught up in how others view me instead of recognizing that my Creator loves me and I don't have to show off to get His attention. I fight to get affirmation from imperfect, sinful people, yet He already loves me with a perfect love. This is such a simple truth, yet we constantly look past it and search for validation from this world.

It breaks my heart to look on social media and see beautiful young girls posting pictures of their nearly naked bodies, just hoping someone will notice them, when their heavenly Father already loves them. As a female, you have probably noticed that guys' minds work differently from ours. Men are extremely visual, so when a girl posts a picture of herself in a bikini, it usually gets a lot of "likes" and comments from guys. This is how God made them, and it isn't going to change. Whether they are Christian guys or not, this is how their brains work. When guys see a woman's cleavage or her panties, even accidentally, their brains start to picture the woman in just those panties or just that bra or sometimes nothing at all. I am being very real with you because we need to protect our brothers in Christ and ourselves. Not only are we hurting guys when we post pictures of ourselves in skimpy clothes, but we are showing the world that we have to stoop to this level to feel good about ourselves. We are saying we need that comment and that "like" to feel wanted. Otherwise, we wouldn't have posted it in the first place.

When I see a girl or a grown woman post a picture like that, I know she is searching for her sacred reflection. God put a longing in our hearts to feel affirmed, wanted, loved, and secure. But we don't need to look to our boyfriends to make us feel loved.

We don't need to post that picture to see if enough people know we are alive. If our husbands or kids are too caught up in their day to see us, it doesn't mean we aren't wanted. Everyone is imperfect, and no person on this earth will be able to show us unconditional love the way our Father God can. When we look to this world for affirmation of our true beauty, we will always be disappointed. The great news is that God will never let us down. If we keep looking to Him and choose to find our worth in Him, we will always be satisfied and will never feel empty.

THE HUSBAND JOURNAL

The summer after I (Megan) was in the ninth grade, we had a girls' lock-in at our church. I remember it distinctly because that was the summer I started my husband journal. You might be thinking, *What in the world is a husband journal?* I am not sure where the idea came from, but I loved it so much I created one at a young age. The journal starts with the attributes you want in a husband: physical, emotional, spiritual… Here's a sample of the attributes or qualities I wanted in a husband:

- Always there for me
- Has goals and achieves them
- A people person
- Crazy about me
- Okay with not always being together

- Compassionate
- Sensitive (sometimes)
- Comforts me when I am down
- Opens doors for me
- Leader, not a follower
- Believes love and marriage are life commitments
- Believes communication is key
- Works hard to make sure we resolve our conflicts
- Listens to me
- Serious when he needs to be
- Patient
- Constantly challenges himself to be better for the Lord
- When making decisions, thinks of us as one person and what is best for both of us
- A gentleman to everyone
- Longs to help the world
- A servant leader
- Constantly encourages me
- Puts God, not me, first in his life
- Compliments me
- Isn't afraid to tell me how he feels, makes himself vulnerable to me

Then the rest of the journal is made up of entries to your future spouse. If you could read some of the things I wrote, you could tell I was a young girl, but I still have the same heart as I did then. I wanted the same things then. I wanted to be loved by someone, someone who loved all of me. I didn't want a perfect guy, one who never made mistakes. I wanted the perfect guy for *me,* a guy who would complement every part of me. I desired to find the true love I saw in my parents and other couples I knew. What I longed for is what every woman longs for—to be loved, cherished, taken care of, and sought after. And not only do we crave to receive this kind of love, but we also want to love someone enough to return the feelings.

Here's one of those entries from my husband journal:

I wonder why I haven't found you yet. I mean, yeah, it's not like I am really old and have been waiting forever, but it's still a valid question. The only possible answers to this question are that I'm not ready, you're not ready, or we both aren't ready. I like the third answer the best because I like knowing we are in this together. But I really don't like thinking that it might be only my fault that I don't have you. I mean, maybe it's stuff God needs to teach me that I really couldn't fix myself, or maybe I know I need to fix some things but I am just being too stubborn. I'm really not sure. Another thing. I really feel like most girls my age aren't overly obsessed with their husbands. No, not boys, husbands. Well, besides my friends. Maybe it's because we are ahead of the game. Or maybe we are trying to stay as close as we can to God and not our flesh, and being obsessed with our husbands sounds better than being obsessed with boys. I mean, we think that sounds more appropriate and godly. Ha, I really don't know. I know it's not bad to love our husbands, but to idolize is bad. What's funny is that I really just idolize the idea of you. I feel that God put such strong feelings on my heart as a good struggle for me but that when I actually get you, I will love you, not idolize you. I need God to show me how to be the best wife possible for you. I need Him to teach me so I can have you and be the perfect match for you. :)

For those of you who are not married, I cannot tell you how surreal it is when you find that one person in the world you've been waiting years for, that one who fits you perfectly. It is mind blowing! I always try to explain to girls who are a little younger than I am that I know how it feels, that I was where they are. I remember that emptiness in the heart because something is missing. Being fully satisfied in your relationship with God places you in the best possible position to see and hear what God has for you. When you don't need a guy to make you happy, when you are relying fully on God for your joy and completeness in this world, then you're ready to *be* the right one and to *find* the right one.

God wants you to know that the hole you feel in your heart is not because you need a man in your life. It's because you need God in your life. Though God has been part of my life since I was a young girl, I still thought I needed a husband to be complete. I was so caught up in my imaginary husband that I took my focus off God. I still loved Him, but because of the distraction of hoping every day my husband would show up and make my life better, I never truly fell in love with God.

I continued my husband journal entries when I went off to college at Baylor University in the fall of 2010. I was positive that my husband was at Baylor and that we would fall in love while we were there and get married, much like my parents' story. To my surprise, my husband was not at Baylor. Two years of college flew by, and not one guy had asked me out! This is when I knew something was wrong with Baylor guys because it obviously wasn't me, right? At this point I realized my husband was not at Baylor and I probably would not find him until after college. If I had known this two years earlier, I would have freaked out. I had always wanted to marry young, and finding my true love at college was a life goal.

So already my overly expectant dreams were crushed. But strangely enough, I was not upset at all. I was actually content. Why? Because my security was not in having a boyfriend or a husband but was grounded in my relationship with God. I was truly excited not to date during the rest of college but to enjoy my friends and experience new things. I loved just having God and depending on no one else. I had found complete joy and happiness in *just* God. It was amazing and so crazy! Even crazier, my husband showed up literally weeks after I decided I didn't need a man in my life. God has quite the sense of humor! Run the race and keep your eye on the prize. Keep running after God. I've been amazed to see God's timing in bringing two people together as husband and wife. It is truly a matter of trusting Him.

Do you desire a godly man who will respect you and treat you like the princess you are? If so, how can you expect that man to come after you when you are dressing and acting to impress an immature boy? That man you are longing for is longing to find a woman of God. Be that woman.

Bold Choices in the Heat of Battle

Choose for yourselves this day whom you will serve.
(Joshua 24:15)

You have choices. You can choose the people you surround yourself with, the guys you date, the one you marry, the way you act, and whom you let validate your beauty. Are you choosing to look in the mirror of peers, culture, or guys? Or in God's mirror? You can choose to be thankful, kind, and loving. It comes down to daily choices. Will you choose to post a selfie because you want people to "like" you, or will you choose to be confident because you know you are already loved? Will you choose to attract attention to yourself or to focus on others? Will you choose to complain about what you don't have or to be thankful for what you do have? Will you choose to focus on your needs and insecurities or to look for a way to brighten someone else's day?

Every day we have to consciously decide to turn to God. Our flesh tells us to focus on ourselves and what we want, but God tells us to focus on Him and others. Ironically, when we take the attention off ourselves, instead of feeling lonely and incomplete, we feel joyful and peaceful. We think it's logical to focus on ourselves if we are feeling unwanted or unnoticed, but that will never fill us up, because that isn't how we were made. God made us to feel content and satisfied only after we have made someone else feel loved.

Fear often determines the choices we make. If we fear not being accepted or our friends not liking us, then we may do something out of character to get their approval.

There is no fear in love. But perfect love drives out fear.
(1 John 4:18)

The opposite of fear is not faith. The opposite of fear is love. The more we look in the mirror of God's unconditional love, the more our insecurities and fears will fade away. The more we realize the truth that our Creator loves us perfectly, the less we'll worry about what everyone else thinks about us.

So the big choice we all have to make every day is to choose love over fear, to boldly live in Christ's love and then boldly reflect His love to others. The irony is, once you start reflecting Christ's love, you'll begin attracting a beautiful team. Not a perfect team but a beautiful team of friends who will encourage you to see your sacred reflection and live from your true beauty.

Reflection

1. After taking the friend test, do you think you need to make some changes? If you do, ask God to give you the courage to stop hanging around people who tear you down rather than build you up.

2. Read 1 John 4:18 (TLB): "We need have no fear of someone who loves us perfectly; his perfect love for us eliminates all dread of what he might do to us. If we are afraid, it is for fear of what he might do to us, and shows that we are not fully convinced that he really loves us." Ask God to fill you with love and to remove your fears. Step out in love today, and risk being a friend to someone who needs encouragement.

Prayer

Lord, I believe there are changes that need to happen in my life. But change is always difficult. At the root of that is one word—fear. I don't want to live in fear, Lord, so give me courage to make those bold choices that will bring me closer to You and Your beautiful plan for my life. I praise You for being the source of perfect love. Amen.

There is no fear in **love**.
But **perfect love** drives
out fear.

1 JOHN 4:18

The Beautiful Rebellion

Don't copy the behavior and customs of this world, but let God transform you into a new person by changing the way you think. Then you will learn to know God's will for you, which is good and pleasing and perfect.

—ROMANS 12:2, NLT

He is no fool who gives what he cannot keep to gain that which he cannot lose.

—JIM ELLIOT

7

Fashion Rebel

Beauty Begins from the Inside Out

You're here to be light, bringing out the
God-colors in the world. God is not a secret
to be kept. We're going public with this, as
public as a city on a hill.

—MATTHEW 5:14, MSG

Everybody wants to make a difference, but
nobody wants to be different. And you
simply cannot have one without the other.

—ANDY ANDREWS

The Urban Dictionary defines a fashion rebel as "someone who doesn't conform to 'what's in' in the fashion world." The funny thing is when a celebrity stands out as a rebel or indie in the fashion world, everyone seems to consider it very fashionable and trendy. Before you know it, the indie fashion is mainstream, and everyone is wearing it. It's conformity and uniformity all over again.

If we really want to be fashion rebels, we first have to rebel against our culture's view that beauty is all about what we look like and wear. The apostle Paul told us that we aren't supposed to fall in line with culture, but we're to be cultural rebels.

Do not conform to the pattern of this world, but be transformed by the renewing of your mind. (Romans 12:2)

The Greek word translated as *conform* literally means to squeeze into a mold.[12] Paul was saying, "Don't let the culture squeeze you into its mold."

Our culture constantly pressures women and girls to fit into a particular mold when it comes to beauty, a mold that destroys our uniqueness and true beauty.

It has been said, "Everyone is born original, but most people die as copies." It's so true!

If we want to live from our sacred reflections and true selves, Paul says we first must let God change the way we think. We must be transformed by the renewing of our minds.

Remember, if we change the way we think, our actions will begin to change. And when our actions change, then our feelings start to change.

GOD'S WARDROBE

If we want to feel beautiful, we need to start by changing the way we think about beauty. Our culture says beauty is all about outward appearance, but Christ says true beauty comes from the inside. So let's fill our minds with this countercultural truth, and we'll make a fashion statement that reveals true beauty.

If you really want to be a fashion rebel, you need to put on the wardrobe God has picked out for you. I just love this passage in Colossians:

> So, chosen by God for this new life of love, dress in the
> wardrobe God picked out for you: compassion, kind-
> ness, humility, quiet strength, discipline. Be even-
> tempered, content with second place, quick to forgive
> an offense. Forgive as quickly and completely as the
> Master forgave you. And regardless of what else you
> put on, wear love. It's your basic, all-purpose garment.
> Never be without it. (3:12–14, MSG)

Did you catch that? God has picked out a wardrobe of character qualities that will perfectly bring out your stunning and true beauty.

How much time do you spend every morning trying to decide what to wear? I have to admit I sometimes try on three or four outfits before I decide. I've always thought, *It must be great to be a guy!* Their choices in clothes are so limited compared to ours. They pick out a shirt and a pair of pants, or maybe they wear a suit to work every day, and about all they need to decide is which tie to wear.

Ladies, when it comes to deciding what to wear and what accessories go with it, our options seem endless. The great news is that when it comes to looking truly beautiful each day, God has already selected the perfect outfits to bring out our inner beauty. So let's take a look at our priceless wardrobe.

A Beautiful Compassion

Colossians tells us the first beautiful quality we're to put on every day is compassion. Jesus wore the clothes of compassion when He walked this earth, as He always looked past the outward appearance of people and saw their inner needs. We're most like Jesus when we get our eyes off ourselves and focus on the person in front of us. Our natural default thinking pattern runs something like this: *Here I am! How do I look? How do I feel? What are you thinking about me?* But true beauty thinks, *There you are! What are your needs? How can I meet them?*

Jesus was clothed with compassion because He always saw into the hearts of hurting people.

> When he went ashore he saw a great crowd, and he
> had compassion on them, because they were like sheep
> without a shepherd. And he began to teach them many
> things. (Mark 6:34, ESV)

The scripture says "he saw . . ." He saw what was really going on in the lives of the people around Him. Likewise, we put on compassion when we take time to truly see people. When we look closely, we'll discover something about each person we encounter: everyone has hidden hurts. We may feel as if we're the only people with scars to hide and struggles to bear, but the truth is just the opposite. When you're hurting, try to remember that someone nearby is hurting too. I've found that I have to be really intentional about this. When I'm especially down or focused inward, I mentally make myself step into someone else's shoes, someone who is going through a rough time.

BEAUTY IN ACTION

The second beautiful outfit we're to wear each day is kindness. This character quality is so much more than niceness. Kindness is really beauty in action.

I'm sure you've heard the axiom "Actions speak louder than words," but the truth is much more harsh. Most actions either completely silence or dramatically magnify what we say. Everything in Scripture points to the fact that our actions matter. A lot. Not because we're trying to earn our way to heaven or gain brownie points with God, but because our actions indicate if Christ is truly living inside us.

> If you have really handed yourself over to Him, it must follow that you are trying to obey Him. But trying in a

new way. . . . Not hoping to get to Heaven as a reward for your actions, but inevitably wanting to act in a certain way because a first faint gleam of Heaven is already inside you.[13]

—C. S. Lewis

For moms, this is an inescapable truth. We spend a sizable chunk of each day trying to teach our children values, manners, and practical life lessons. "Chew with your mouth closed." "Reading is great." "Be grateful for what you have." "Eat your vegetables." "Don't text and drive." "Share." "Don't complain." "You're beautiful just as you are." "It's what's on the inside that counts."

But what if my daughter never sees me reading? What if she catches me checking my e-mail at a stoplight? And what if she sees me looking critically in the mirror, complaining that my hair is too frizzy, my hips are too wide, or my nose is too big?

The most important lessons in life are caught, not taught. Our kids follow in the footsteps we thought we'd covered up. Mothers who make negative comments about their own looks inadvertently teach their daughters to turn that critical mirror on themselves.

If we want to be beautiful—and what woman doesn't?—

the secret is found in Ephesians 5:1 (NLT): "Imitate God." True beauty is God without disguise. The more His love shows up in our actions, the more beautiful we'll be.

It's not enough to have kind thoughts. A great thought means nothing without actions. We're called to beautiful actions. To risk rejection. To risk looking foolish. To bare our hearts and risk their breaking.

Colossians 3:12 goes on to list the beautiful accessories of humility, quiet strength, and discipline that we need to wear every day. These character qualities can all be summed up with the next verse: "Be even-tempered, content with second place" (MSG).

Talk about a countercultural fashion statement. The loudest voices in our culture say, "Be first! Look out for yourself! Be noticed!" Really, we're never more beautiful than when we lift others up and make them feel beautiful. As C. S. Lewis said, a humble man "will not be thinking about humility: he will not be thinking about himself at all."[14]

True beauty starts with focusing on others. Not on our hair, clothes, or abs, but on others. And as much as we might like to sometimes, we can't skip over the people we live with—parents, children, brothers, sisters, husbands. They are where the rubber meets the road as far as beautiful actions are concerned.

THE BEAUTY OF FORGIVENESS

The Bible also reminds us to wear the beautiful quality of forgiveness. In this world we will experience deep hurts, but every day we have a choice to put on the ugly garment of bitterness or the beautiful coat of forgiveness.

Maybe the first person you need to forgive before you can wear the wardrobe of Christlike character is your mother. I (Chris) hope your mother was like mine, a wonderful example of true inner beauty. I know, however, that is not always the case. Maybe your mother neglected you or never made you feel loved. You may have some deep hurts caused by the one who was supposed to be your first example of true beauty. But we need to accept that every mom makes mistakes. None of us was raised by a perfect mom. That's why it's so important to forgive.

In *Forgiving Our Fathers and Mothers: Finding Freedom from Hurt and Hate,* authors Leslie Leyland Fields and Dr. Jill Hubbard state:

> It is not a simple thing to do this, to see beyond the roles our mothers and fathers at least partially failed at. To see beyond our need for them to their larger selves. But they were always more than our mothers and fathers. If you have children yourself, you know the truth of this, how

much our children don't know about us. How much of
ourselves we hold back. Don't we know that our own
parents were boys and girls, with parents themselves
and siblings and a kitchen sink with a leaky faucet and
a sickly brother and a teacher they disliked and a secret
hideout in their attic? And if they married, they did so
with dreams and hopes for good lives, better lives than
they were given in their own first homes. And when
your mother birthed you, she may have wept with joy.
And if she gave you to someone else, to another set of
parents, she may have wept with grief. Your father may
remember the day you were born as the best day of his
life.[15]

Isn't that so true? How often we forget that our mothers
were little girls at one time. Again, that doesn't excuse the short-
comings of their adult lives, but it can shed some light of understanding. And maybe in that light, forgiveness can begin. Will
that be a miraculous, instantaneous experience where everyone
will hug and kiss and make up and be fully restored? Because
of the kind of God we serve, yes, that's possible. But the more
probable scenario is that the God we serve will allow us to experience the way forgiveness usually works—one step and one
word at a time.

What if your mother has passed away? As much as you

might like to work toward forgiveness between her and you, it's just you.

> Be kind and compassionate to one another, forgiving each other, just as in Christ God forgave you. (Ephesians 4:32)

Author Brennan Manning had a tumultuous relationship with his mother. It is recounted in pieces in his memoir *All Is Grace.* In this passage Manning contends that a trusting heart is forgiven and, in turn, forgives and that a trusting heart is also a beautiful heart.

> I know that's true because of an experience I had on a November day in 2003. My mother had been dead and gone for close to ten years. As I was praying about other things, her face flashed across the window of my mind. It was not a worn face like that of an old mother or grandmother, but a child's face. I saw my mother as a little six-year-old girl kneeling on the windowsill of the orphanage in Montreal. Her nose was pressed against the glass; she was begging God to send her a mommy and daddy who would whisk her away and love her without condition. As I looked, I believe I finally *saw*

my mother; she was a ragamuffin too. And all my resentment and anger fell away.

The little girl turned and walked toward me. As she drew closer, the years flew by and she stood before me an aged woman. She said, "You know, I messed up a lot when you were a kid. But you turned out okay." Then my old mother did something she'd never done before in her life, never once. She kissed me on the lips and on both cheeks. At that moment I knew that the hurt between my mother and me was real and did matter, but that it was okay. The trusting heart gives a second chance; it is forgiven and, in turn, forgives. I looked at my mother and said, "I forgive you." She smiled and said, "I guess sometimes you do get what you ask for."[16]

EXTRAVAGANT LOVE

Last, but definitely not least, we are always to put on the beautiful garment of love, the quality that, like a diamond, has so many facets.

And regardless of what else you put on, wear love. It's your basic, all-purpose garment. Never be without it. (Colossians 3:14, MSG)

The most beautiful Christlike characteristic we can reflect to others is love. Love is that classic, timeless, and beautiful fashion statement that holds the power to change everything. Jesus constantly demonstrated extravagant love that shocked the prideful and brought beauty to the broken all around Him.

EXTRAVAGANT LIVING

> When a certain immoral woman from that city heard he [Jesus] was eating there, she brought a beautiful alabaster jar filled with expensive perfume. Then she knelt behind him at his feet, weeping. Her tears fell on his feet, and she wiped them off with her hair. Then she kept kissing his feet and putting perfume on them. (Luke 7:37–38, NLT)

The woman displayed extravagant love. She opened up a very expensive jar of perfume, probably her most valuable possession in the world, and she poured out the perfume. As it splashed on Jesus's feet, it mixed with something even more precious, her tears of repentance. She was accused of being wasteful. She was accused of being extravagant. Wasteful she was not. But she was extravagant. Yes, she was extravagant, but she experienced extravagant forgiveness. She experienced extravagant emotional healing. She experienced extravagant love and peace.

I (Chris) am convinced more and more that the only way to build rich and deep relationships is with extravagance. If I'm going to connect on a deep level with my kids, it will take extravagant effort. I have to get into their lives. It takes extravagant creativity and energy and effort, but sometimes I settle for a "just enough" kind of effort and creativity.

To continue a deep and strong relationship with my husband takes extravagant intentionality. We have to get out our calendars and plan our dates and our getaways. We have to plan time in our busy schedules for conversation so we can connect on a deep level. We have to be intentional about keeping our marriage strong and deep.

A relationship that lasts a lifetime requires extravagant forgiveness because imperfect people are going to hurt each other, and those wounds need more than a band-aid.

Building and maintaining deep relationships demands extravagant commitment, extravagant intentionality, extravagant energy, extravagant creativity, extravagant forgiveness, extravagant love, and extravagant effort.

I'm not talking about extravagance on the outside. I'm talking about extravagance from the heart, the deepest part of who we are. The "immoral woman" extravagantly poured out her heart before Jesus Christ. The expensive perfume was just a symbol of her heart, which was so precious and valuable. Her tears mingled with the perfume and created the most beautiful fragrance of all—the fragrance of a beautiful heart.

Do you have a beautiful heart? This woman had a broken heart, but she poured her heart out before Christ, and He made it beautiful. Pour your heart out before Christ, and let Him fill you with the beauty of His extravagant love for you.

Today make the intentional choice to be a fashion rebel and put on God's wardrobe. Let's decide daily to put on the beautiful character qualities of Christ and let Him change us from the inside out.

Reflection

1. Read Colossians 3:12–14 (MSG) again: "So, chosen by God for this new life of love, dress in the wardrobe God picked out for you: compassion, kindness, humility, quiet strength, discipline. Be even-tempered, content with second place, quick to forgive an offense. Forgive as quickly and completely as the Master forgave you. And regardless of what else you put on, wear love. It's your basic, all-purpose garment. Never be without it." Which part of God's wardrobe do you most often forget to wear? Pray and ask God to strengthen this character quality in your life.

2. Whom have you *seen* today? Not just looked at, but truly seen, listened to, and felt compassion for? The phrase "Practice random acts of kindness" was popular for a season, but like most things it has faded. Although the thought behind it was good, the phrase suffered from the word *random*. No, kindness has to be intentional. What can you decide to do today that is kind? Remember, you're not trying to save the world; you're simply trying to love the one in front of you.

Prayer

Lord, of all the things I put on each and every day, help me not to leave the house without putting on those qualities that reflect You, especially the foundation—love. Teach me to love extravagantly in every aspect of my life, from the inside out, and to be intentional about it. Amen.

Imitate God, therefore, in **everything** you do, because **you** are his dear children.

EPHESIANS 5:1, NLT

8

Cultural Revolution

Beauty Begins When Complacency Ends

What good is it for someone to gain the
whole world, yet forfeit their soul?

—MARK 8:36

I have one desire now—to live a life of
reckless abandon for the Lord, putting all
my energy and strength into it.

—ELISABETH ELLIOT

When Malala Yousafzai was eleven years old, she began writing a blog, using a fake name, that detailed her life growing up in the Swat Valley of Pakistan under Taliban occupation. Malala wrote about the destructive extremist culture that looked down on girls getting an education and at times banned them from attending school altogether. Soon she began to speak openly about her views promoting education for girls in the Swat Valley, and as she did, she gained more media attention, especially in Pakistan but also internationally.

A few years later as Malala was riding the school bus one

day, a man got on the bus, asked for her by name, and then pulled out a gun and shot her in the forehead. Malala somehow survived the vicious attack and went through multiple surgeries and months of rehabilitation. The news of this cowardly act against such a courageous young girl made headlines around the world and rallied people to Malala's cause. Her courage in standing against the extremists in her culture and for the education of young girls started a movement, which is gaining steam.

In 2014 Malala became the youngest person to receive the Nobel Peace Prize. She continues to speak for young girls who have been oppressed in her culture and around the world. I'm sure she didn't set out to start a revolution against the lies in her culture that were devastating young girls. She just took her stand, and the rest is history.[17]

Like Malala, we must take our stand against the lies in our culture that are being forced on young girls. We may not experience physical danger, as Malala did, but every day we experience emotional damage that is destroying the self-esteem of millions of beautiful young women.

Women are waking up to the fact that we've been looking in the distorted mirror of our culture for far too long. Let's courageously choose to stand against the lies of the Enemy and look in the mirror of God's truth and live from our sacred reflections. Let's choose to stand together in God's power and grace. Maybe together we can start a revolution that changes the mirror of our culture and reflects the beauty of Christ.

DARE TO BE DIFFERENT

This revolution in our culture will require radical changes. If you want to feel like most women today—that you will never measure up to an insane, distorted view of beauty—then do what they are doing. But if you long to feel what God feels about you and live from your true beauty, then you have to stop doing what everyone else is doing and make some radical changes.

"Although I don't want to do it, I'm just going to make these people happy." That's what Colbie Caillat said to Kenneth "Babyface" Edmonds as she stepped into the recording studio. The Grammy Award–winner and singer-songwriter was getting pressure to change herself and conform to a widely accepted image of beauty, one in which the nails are always exquisite, the outfit is simply the best, and the hair and makeup all look perfect.

But the truth, according to Caillat, "is that I like myself when I'm not that way." In a moment of countercultural encouragement, Babyface urged her to stand her ground and shine a light on the enormous pressure to change. The result was Caillat's collaborative effort with Babyface and Jason Reeves—"Try."

Take your makeup off . . .
Don't you like you?[18]

For the "Try" video, Caillat didn't do prep work like starving herself or exercising like mad. She didn't get her hair and nails done. She didn't get a facial. She didn't even have a stylist (what?!). And on the album cover for *Gypsy Heart*, she refused to let them touch up her picture. She went completely natural, and "Try" became her highest charting single in Australia and Canada in five years. The accompanying video has now been viewed millions of times.[19]

I'm not saying you need to stop wearing makeup. I'm saying if you want to stop the insanity of never feeling beautiful, you have to stop doing what everyone else is doing.

LIVE A RADICAL LIFE

Do you want to live a life that matters? You can. Do you want to stand out from the crowd and live the life you dream of? Then do it! Be different. Be radical. Be who you were made to be. When we say, "Let's be radical," we're really saying, "Let's return to our roots." What is radical to this world is normal to

God. The early New Testament Christians lived radical lives. How did they do this? They embraced the radical love and the power of God with "reckless abandon." Radical became normal for them—healing the blind, raising the dead, and winning thousands of hearts. These people risked everything because they knew that Jesus loved them completely, had a plan for them, and wanted to do something radical through them.

They changed the world but not because they were extraordinary and had amazing talents. No. They were ordinary. They had ordinary faith and ordinary abilities just like you and me.

They chose, however, to place all their ordinary faith in an extraordinary God, who did extraordinary things through them. God always uses ordinary, imperfect people to fulfill His plans. But we must be ordinary people who totally surrender to His extraordinary love. We also have to take our ordinary, imperfect faith and place it all in His extraordinary and perfect power.

I admit that I don't have the strength to swim against the powerful current of our culture that seeks to sweep away my self-worth with its lies. I don't have the courage to live a radical life that rebels against the tidal wave of pressure to conform to what everyone else is doing.

The good news is I don't have to have that kind of strength and courage. All I need to do is turn to the One who does have the strength and courage.

Remember, "I can do all things through Christ who strengthens me" (Philippians 4:13, NKJV). All things? Yes. That means if I turn to Christ, He will give me the strength to stand up and rebel against the lies of our culture. With God's power I can stop looking at myself in the mirror with a critical eye, and I can start living from my sacred reflection. With God's strength I can stop overemphasizing what's on the outside and start focusing on having beautiful character on the inside.

Just imagine for a moment what would happen if we started a revolution in beauty, a revolution that would bring the healing power of Christ's love to millions of women who are longing for their sacred reflections. I know it seems impossible that we can change our culture. But don't ever forget the words of Jesus: "With people this is impossible, but with God all things are possible" (Matthew 19:26, NASB).

ONE-EIGHTY-DEGREE REVOLUTION

Repent, for the kingdom of heaven has come near.
(Matthew 3:2)

That was the message John the Baptist preached in the wilderness of Judea. When we hear that word *repent,* most of us think it means we should feel sorry for something, possibly even regretful. That's unfortunate, because when the Bible uses that word, it means to turn around 180 degrees, to experience a profound change in the way we think, feel, and live. That's what we need when it comes to beauty—to repent, to turn 180 degrees, and to point to something completely different, something beyond the surface of our accepted cultural definitions. We need to do beauty differently.

> A repentant heart is open to God, intimately connected with him, always living in the light of the truth, and free to radically love others without regret or limitation![20]
> —Sharon Hersh

I need to do a 180-degree turn from trying to look beautiful to seeking to live beautifully. I have to say "enough" to my selfish focus and choose to be part of a selfless revolution.

REAL SUPERMODELS

We see pictures of supermodels and try to look like them even though most of those pictures have been enhanced. Instead, we should do a one-eighty and stop trying to look like the supermodels on magazine covers and start imitating the real supermodels, those who model true beauty. They are all around us.

They just don't clamor for attention by what they wear. You'll find them, not on the runway, but in your neighborhood or in your church, beautifully reflecting Christ's love in the real world.

The most beautiful women I know are those who focus on making everyone around them feel beautiful. The small things they do for others and the way they live make such an impact and portray such beauty.

When I (Megan) was a senior in high school, Ms. Thomas was my English teacher. Although I'll try to describe her, she is one of those ladies you need to meet in person because words alone don't do her justice. She's taught school for decades, but her enthusiasm for helping students succeed hasn't dwindled at all. In fact, it may be even greater now than when she started. Ms. Thomas brought to life every novel we were assigned, and she made every project and assignment enjoyable.

Most days my friends and I would stay after class just to talk with Ms. Thomas about life. She never made us feel that we were a nuisance; instead, she treated us as people she was genuinely interested in. Her enthusiasm was infectious. She seemed to enjoy everything about English but also everything about life. Her challenge to me was to "be all there," to be fully present in every moment of every day. There was no question whether Ms. Thomas believed in God. The way she talked, acted, and loved was all the evidence we needed of her faith.

The bottom line is she was kind, and therefore she was beautiful. I honestly don't remember any of the clothes she wore or what makeup she used. But I vividly remember how her kindness made me feel.

> They may forget what you said, but they will never
> forget how you made them feel.[21]
> —Carl W. Buehner

I (Megan) think it's very important for women my age to find wise mentors who have been through a lot of the things we're going through now. The most beautiful women I know are much older than I am, but they reflect the beauty of wisdom that transcends generations.

Dominique Browning wrote an article for the *New York Times* titled "I'm Too Old for This." From where she sits now, Browning laments the self-criticism about her appearance that accompanied so much of her growing-up years, when nothing ever felt quite right. In one poignant story she shares about recently coming across a trunk that had been locked for years. Here is what she found:

> It was full of photographs. There I was, ages 4 to 40.
> And I saw for the first time that even when I was in the
> depths of despair about my looks, I had been beautiful.

And there were all my friends. . . . We were, we are, all beautiful. Just like our mothers told us, or should have. (Ahem.)

Those smiles, radiant with youth, twinkled out of the past, reminding me of the smiles I know today, radiant with strength.

Young(er) women, take this to heart: Why waste time and energy on insecurity? I have no doubt that when I'm 80 I'll look at pictures of myself when I was 60 and think how young I was then, how filled with joy and beauty.[22]

Young women can't always accept this perspective and take Browning's words to heart. Sometimes a person simply needs to live awhile to have a context for these things. But no one should look down on you because you're young. We not only need beautiful mentors, but we also should look for women we can encourage.

A HIVE OF ENCOURAGEMENT

All sorrows can be borne if you put them into a story or tell a story about them.[23]

—Isak Dinesen

One of the prominent themes in Sue Monk Kidd's best-selling novel *The Secret Life of Bees* is sisterhood, the life-giving power that resides in a community of women. Of the quote above, the author said:

> Ever since I first read that line, I've carried it with me. When women bond together in a community in such a way that "sisterhood" is created, it gives them an accepting and intimate forum to tell their stories and have them heard and validated by others. The community not only helps to heal their circumstance, but encourages them to grow into their larger destiny.[24]

We need each other, and we need to bring about a revolution of encouragement. So many things in our culture can be extremely discouraging to women, but we can be rebels of encouragement. Lavish encouragement on the women closest to you. Speak encouragement into the lives of those around you. Write encouraging notes and cards. Show the beauty of encouragement.

> We aren't called to relate to the culture; we're called to revolutionize the culture.[25]
>   —Matthew Burnett

REVOLUTIONARY WRITING

One of the most beautiful gifts I (Chris) have ever received was a letter Megan gave me on the Mother's Day before she went to college. I want to share it with you here:

Hey, Mom, I just want to wish you a happy Mother's Day! I want to let you know I love and appreciate you so much, and I couldn't ask for a more loving mom. The thing I admire most about you is that you've shown me how to love other people. I see that most clearly in your relationship with Dad and how much you guys appreciate each other and enjoy each other's company. I know there are days when I get really frustrated and annoyed and I'm in a horrible mood, but even then you make the effort to tell me how much you love me. You make sure you do this before I leave the house, and it's always with a hug and a kiss as well. For the past few years my relationship with God has really grown, and I know you've noticed that, and you've helped me with any questions I've had. More important, you've shown me a consistent example by reading your Bible and having your own quiet time during the day. I've noticed you too, and that's the kind of woman I want to be. I know I'm going off to college soon and I'm your only girl, and that makes you kind of sad. But please know that I won't forget what you've taught me, and I'll be only three hours away. You know I'll be calling you a lot too. Mom, again I hope you have a very happy Mother's Day. I love you so much!

I've made a lot of mistakes as a mom, but that letter made me feel so treasured. Whom do you need to write a note to today? Your mom? A teacher? A friend?

Let's start a radical cultural revolution of encouragement that makes the women around us feel beautiful. That's the only way we can recognize our own true beauty.

Reflection

1. Read Philippians 4:13 (NKJV): "I can do all things through Christ who strengthens me." What do you need to do to stand against the lies in our culture? Ask God to be your strength to stand.

2. Think about the older women who are mentors in your life. Is their presence consistent? Occasional? Seldom? Now consider the younger women in your life that you mentor, and ask yourself the same question.

Prayer

Lord, forgive the complacency so often present in my life. Show me those places where I need to do a one-eighty and turn toward You and others. Thank You so much for the ways You have encouraged me in the past and continue to encourage me to this day. Help me in turn to encourage other women, to do my part in Your beautiful revolution. Amen.

I can do **all things** through
Christ who **strengthens** me.

PHILIPPIANS 4:13, NKJV

9

A Beautiful Legacy

Beauty Begins and Never Ends

Generation after generation stands in awe
of your work;
each one tells stories of your mighty acts.

—Psalm 145:4, MSG

Some people, no matter how old they get,
never lose their beauty. They merely move
it from their faces into their hearts.

—Martin Buxbaum

This verse from Psalms tells us two things. First, we are encouraged to tell the next generation about God's mighty acts. It's a practice that inspires awe and praise in those who hear. Second, the ways in which God has intervened in and redeemed *your* story need to be told; it's what people used to refer to as a personal testimony.

Maybe you're thinking, *You don't know my story. It's full of bad characters and loose ends.* Maybe you're waiting till you get your act together so you'll have something worth sharing. Did you forget that a great story is never predictable and perfect? Who'd want to read that? Every great story is, at the heart, a story of overcoming. Make no mistake. God is writing your story, even this very minute. The Master Storyteller chose what decade you'd be born in, what country you'd live in, and who your parents would be.

The trouble is that we spend most of our years wishing we weren't in them. As teenagers we want to look, act, and have the privileges that come with being twentysomethings. When we're in our twenties, we realize that being of working age brings with it a lot of responsibility—brutal college exams, job searches, long workdays, housing and utility bills, car payments. Who asked for this? We're now the target of huge ad campaigns for clothes and makeup, but it's so stressful to have to pay for it all! So we set our eyes on the next decade, hoping we'll morph into a cover girl. By the time we're in our thirties and forties, most of us long for those carefree years of our teens and twenties. With stretch marks and the first gray hairs comes the struggle to look young again. As our wrinkles deepen in our fifties and sixties, we realize we have a condition that nothing on this earth can fix—namely, bodies that are wearing out like old clothes.

But here's the good news. You are not your body! Your body is just an earth suit, a container for your spirit, the real you.

Imagine that I have placed two coffee cups in front of you. One is a delicate cup that is hand painted with gorgeous flowers and trimmed in twenty-four-karat gold. The other is an old, cheap souvenir that is smudged with dirt and chipped on the rim.

Choose one.

Oh wait. Before you pick, let me mention what's inside. The coffee in the pretty cup has a couple of tablespoons of raw sewage mixed into it. The junky cup is filled with steaming hot, world-class coffee.

I can hear you yelling, "That bad cup is all mine!" I'm with you. In fact a hundred out of a hundred women would agree it's what's inside the cup that matters. There's nothing inherently wrong with owning or using a nice cup, as long as you understand that it doesn't improve the coffee. If the coffee isn't good, it doesn't matter how great the cup is. The outside is totally unrelated to what's on the inside.

For some reason we have trouble transferring this simple principle to our lives. Our bodies are just the cups that hold our true selves. It's absurd that we spend our lives worrying about how our cups look! The problem is that our perspective has been all wrong.

We don't *have* to age. We *get* to age.

What time and experience do to our outsides is irrelevant. It's how time and experience affect our insides that counts.

Why is it easy for us to recognize this principle everywhere but in our own lives?

The truth is that beauty is abundant in every stage of life. The world, not knowing any better, champions beauty's counterfeit: mere prettiness. People spend their lives hoping that someone will look at them and say, "Wow, that's a nice cup!"

So it's scary when the odds of that happening decrease with every year. It reminds me of a certain hamster our family used to have. Snowball spent a good chunk of each day running on his wheel, and it always seemed to go a little faster than he did. Snowball would trot happily along, but the wheel would start coming toward him in a blur. He'd gradually speed up until finally he'd break into an all-out run. On and on he'd go until he was exhausted. Then he'd stumble off in exactly the same place he'd started. He was addicted to the wheel.

Do you ever feel like that hamster? I know I do! Sometimes I try and try to fit in, measure up, and be pretty, but at the end of the day, I'm exhausted and no further ahead. That's definitely not the life God planned for you and me. In fact, it's the opposite. Read this next passage slowly. Let it sink in.

> Are you tired? Worn out? Burned out on religion?
> Come to me. Get away with me and you'll recover
> your life. I'll show you how to take a real rest. Walk
> with me and work with me—watch how I do it.
> Learn the unforced rhythms of grace. (Matthew
> 11:28–29, MSG)

THE KEY SECRET

Do you want to know what real beauty looks like? Picture Mother Teresa. Her complexion was etched with too-deep lines—the scars of a lifetime of caring, laughter, and heartfelt tears. Her teeth were yellowing and a little crooked. Her hair wasn't set in the latest style. In fact, it wasn't on display at all. Her body was tiny and frail. The only feature that was truly arresting was her eyes. Not because they were overly large or a striking color or framed by long lashes, but because they were filled with piercing love.

Defying all odds, the woman I just described is universally thought to be beautiful. You see, every once in a while a woman comes along whose inner life overshadows her outward shell. Untold billions of dollars are spent each year to make bodies appear younger and more beautiful. How crazy is it that a tiny Albanian woman living alongside some of the poorest and least powerful people on the planet discovered the secret to beauty?

Mother Teresa's beauty secrets can't be found on any garish billboards or in blaring commercials. They were whispered by a smiling little old woman with an Albanian accent.

Lean in and listen:

We are called upon not to be successful, but to be faithful.[26]

If we have no peace, it is because we have forgotten that we belong to each other.[27]

No one thinks of the pen while reading a letter. They only want to know the mind of the person who wrote the letter. That's exactly what I am in God's hand—a little pencil. God is writing his love letter to the world in this way, through works of love.[28]

It is easy to love the people far away. It is not always easy to love these close to us. It is easier to give a cup of rice to relieve hunger than to relieve the loneliness and pain of someone unloved in our own home. Bring love into your home, for this is where our love for each other must start.[29]

If you remove Jesus from my life, my life is reduced to a mere nothing.[30]

Did you catch that? The secret is *free*! It's ours for the taking! So why aren't we following Mother Teresa's example? The ugly truth is, we don't like the answer. We want a cream or a pill or a treatment that will fix us. We want something that will require our dollars but not our souls. Something that will shape our hair, thighs, or eyebrows but leave our hearts as stubborn as ever. Our spirits long for dye, and we settle for paint.

Mother Teresa's earthly life ended in 1997, but her influence continues to be powerful and relevant. That's how it is with real beauty. Beauty begins with the way you live, not what you look like. If you choose to live beautifully, your beauty will never die. Like ripples from a stone dropped in a pond, your example will resonate through generations.

On the other hand, if your life revolves around yourself, the exact opposite is true. If your biggest concern is how you appear to others, you will end up living a very small life. Any prettiness you attained in life will die with you. The Bible puts it this way:

> The person who plants selfishness, ignoring the needs
> of others . . . harvests a crop of weeds. All he'll have to
> show for his life is weeds! (Galatians 6:8, MSG)

The amazing thing is that Jesus offers His whole self to us. His mind, His power, His wisdom, His perspective, and His patience—they're all ours if we choose moment by moment to let His light shine through us.

BEAUTIFUL FEET

In Romans 10:15, Paul reminds us, "How beautiful are the feet of those who bring good news!" That verse has always seemed strange to me. Maybe how beautiful is the mouth or eyes, but feet? They're not usually on the list of best body parts. In fact, in the survey we mentioned earlier, not a single woman or girl listed feet as a coveted attribute. Feet are usually the dirtiest part of our bodies. That's what makes this verse so interesting. Paul calls feet beautiful because of what they *do,* not because of what they *look like.* If Christ lives in you, you are a light. If your feet carry you to shine your light on others, they are beautiful.

God clearly operates from a different definition of beauty, and this verse reveals the heart of it. Our body parts are beautiful to the degree they're used for His purposes. Your feet are beautiful when they carry you to your neighbors' house to comfort them in their grief, or when they lead you to a nursing home to visit the lonely, or when they kick a soccer ball with the neighborhood kids. Your hands are beautiful when you wipe a toddler's runny nose, prepare a meal to share, or write a note of encouragement to a friend who lost his job. Your arms are beautiful when they are wrapped around a sick child or are raking an elderly neighbor's yard. Your mouth is beautiful when it smiles at a stranger, speaks words of kindness, and stays closed until you have something good to say. Your eyes are beautiful when they see the hidden needs of others, recognize the fingerprints of God, and look for beauty in unlikely places. Your ears are beautiful when they listen to an old woman telling stories, hear the unspoken plea in a teenager's words, and shut out the noise of the world in order to listen for that still, small voice.

Everything God made has unlimited potential for beauty. But it never comes from the outside in. The moment we focus on being outwardly beautiful, we're not. However, when we use ourselves for His purposes, beauty is a natural by-product.

Ironically, we're the most beautiful when we no longer care if we are beautiful. In fact, when we aren't thinking of ourselves at all!

MAKE YOUR CHOICE

Imagine that I just said you've won the grand prize in a lottery and will get to choose one of two homes to live in. I hold up two keys and take you to select your new home. There are two houses side by side. The one on the left has loads of curb appeal and catches your eye right away. It has a fresh coat of paint, charming gables and shutters, and flowerpots brimming with daisies. The lawn is immaculate. Neatly trimmed hedges line the perfectly edged walkway. You eagerly walk to the front door and put the key in the gleaming lock.

As you step through the door, the first thing that hits you is the smell. It's an unsettling mixture of rotting garbage, dog poop, and old sneakers. As your eyes adjust to the dimly lit room, the details are revealed. The floor is grimy, cracked, and seems to slant to one side. The ceiling is sagging and stained. Further inspection reveals leaky plumbing and broken appliances. The only signs of life are swarms of cockroaches scurrying on the floorboards as you enter each room. Eager to step back into the daylight, you grab my hand and pull me outside. As we retrace our steps past the glossy exterior, you wonder aloud how such a stunning facade could be attached to such a pit.

Next you turn toward the house next door. Though it's well kept, there's nothing flashy about this one, but it has a simple dignity. The paint is rather worn, and the geraniums on the porch are starting to wilt. A hopscotch game drawn in chalk hasn't quite faded from the front walk. A few stray toys are scattered on the porch. A book is lying open on the rocking chair by the front door next to a half-full glass of tea. The doormat is worn from years of welcomes. You step inside and feel, well, at home. Everything is lived in and well cared for. The floors are clean and glowing, the hearth is tidy, and good smells are coming from the kitchen. Everything reflects a sense of stability, order, warmth, and welcome.

Two keys. Two houses. The choice is yours. It's a decision we make over and over every day because our bodies are the houses we live in.

Therefore, I urge you, brothers and sisters, in view of God's mercy, to offer your bodies as a living sacrifice, holy and pleasing to God—this is your true and proper worship. (Romans 12:1)

DAILY DECISION

We get to choose our legacy, but it's not a one-time decision. Our lives are made up of thousands of little decisions. We can spend our days trying to maintain our exteriors, or we can give our lives away and gain new interiors in the process.

Grandma Edie was one of the greatest beauties I (Chris) have ever known. She grew up on a working farm in Illinois and always stayed true to her roots. She sported a simple, no-nonsense haircut that looked the same whether she had just come in from her daily three-mile walk or was reading a book to her grandchildren. She did her laundry in an ancient crank machine in her basement. When asked why she didn't get a modern automatic washer, she said, "This one works just fine, and I have the time. Why would I replace it?" I never saw her with any makeup on. Ever. Grandma Edie didn't dress to impress or distract. She was too focused on others to worry about what they were thinking of her.

If you had passed my grandma on the street, you probably wouldn't have noticed her or taken the time to get to know her, and that would have been your great loss. You see, if you had spent ten minutes with Grandma Edie, you would have discovered more wisdom, common sense, joy, and laughter than you'd find in a lifetime with most people. And even though she's been in heaven for many years, she still impacts my life every day. She had the kind of beauty that truly makes a difference.

When my time on earth has come and gone, I don't care if anyone remembers what I looked like. But I hope it will be said that . . .

I smiled into the future.

I saw the world's needs and tried my best to fill them.

I ran toward people in pain instead of running away from them.

I celebrated others' joy as if it were my own.

I held up a mirror that reflected God's image and said, "*This* is who you are! I see the Beautiful One's fingerprints all over you."

> She is clothed with strength and dignity;
> > she can laugh at the days to come. (Proverbs 31:25)

WE NEED EACH OTHER

I'll admit it. There are plenty of days when I see a herd of women stampeding to a place called Pretty, and I jump in, worried that I'll be left behind. I get so busy trying to make it to Pretty that I forget it's not where I was headed. I desperately need to be surrounded by like-minded women. Not perfect women. Just some ladies who are headed in the same direction.

Here's the truth: as we get older, the physical is stripped away, exposing more of who we really are. It's a sobering thought. Whatever spirit we've nurtured throughout our lives will be revealed more clearly with age. These cocoons we live in will someday become utterly useless. How tragic if we spend our lives painting our cocoons and emerge as withered worms in the end.

To get an accurate picture of who God is and who we are to the next generation, we have to realize that we're not in a cocoon competition. Let's encourage one another to boldly embrace whatever age and stage we find ourselves in. We're in it by design, you know.

It's not too late. Your story is still being written. The Master Storyteller is at work. As you lean into the story, everything around you will melt away. Before you know it, you'll forget the worries and distractions that weigh you down. You'll forget your surroundings, and soon you'll even forget yourself, till at last only the story will remain.

Join us. Step into the journey to beautiful. You're no longer on the outside looking in. No, you're part of the story.

Reflection

1. If you want to leave a beautiful legacy, you have to get intentional about it. First Thessalonians 4:7 (MSG) tells us, "God hasn't invited us into a disorderly, unkempt life but into something holy and beautiful—as beautiful on the inside as the outside." What do you want your legacy to be? Be specific.

2. What changes do you need to make in your habits and schedule to start living that legacy today?

Prayer

Lord, I know we can't truly save time but can only spend it. So help me in the hundreds of little decisions I make each day to choose wisely and bravely, for those decisions all add up to determine how I will be remembered. And I want to be remembered not for how I looked but for how I loved. I want people to say of me, "She was one who could laugh at the days to come." Amen.

She is clothed with **strength** and **dignity**;
she can **laugh** at the days to come.

PROVERBS 31:25

Addendum

A Challenge To Men

By Kerry Shook and Jordan Alpha

> Husbands, go all out in your love for
> your wives, exactly as Christ did for the
> church—a love marked by giving, not
> getting.
>
> —Ephesians 5:25, msg

> Fathers, be good to your daughters
> Daughters will love like you do.
>
> —John Mayer

This is not our book. But we were asked to contribute a chapter, one addressed to the husbands and fathers and sons out there who've had, have, or will have a place in a woman's life. We realize many female voices today are saying, "I don't need a man in my life to define me." And you know what? They're right. The thought that we could somehow give Chris or Megan her identity is absolutely silly. That comes from God and God alone. These ladies are both strong, independent women living out the call God has placed on their lives. No, we have no illusions of defining them, but we have tried, to the best of our ability and with God's help, to delight in them and help them see their true beauty. And we hope that has made a difference along the way.

The Biggest Fan

When Megan was five years old, Chris and I (Kerry) went to a restaurant that had a live band playing. In the middle of dinner, I looked up to see Megan dancing her heart out right next to the band. She was the only one in the entire restaurant dancing, and when I say *dancing,* I mean *dancing.* She had the biggest smile on her face and was completely unconcerned about what anyone else was thinking about her or her moves. Megan was totally in the moment, and that image will never leave my heart because it was a moment of pure delight, both for Megan and for me as her father. If I hadn't realized it before, I knew then that I was to be Megan's biggest fan and that I wanted her to be able to dance like that or sing like that or cheer like that or simply live like that—with reckless abandon—as she grew into a woman.

Be one of her true believers. Be the person in your girl's life who is wildly optimistic about her chances for success. Concentrate on all her good qualities.

Be sickeningly optimistic and energized, carbonated
beyond recognition! Blast her with hope![31]
    —William and Kathryn Beausay

Fathers, our daughters need to know that we are their biggest fans. That no matter where they are or what music is playing or who else chooses to dance or not, we are delighted in and
with them. Consider all the things we men typically are fans
of—sports teams, a certain brand of truck, maybe a singer or a
band. Now consider how we men typically demonstrate we are
fans. We paint our faces or our bellies, spend hours washing and
waxing and detailing those trucks, or pay better than good
money for tickets close to the stage. Do we fathers typically demonstrate that same level of enthusiasm for our daughters? I wish
I could give a resounding yes! But I'm afraid I can't. Sure, there
may be moments here and there, on occasion, but do our daughters know daily, consistently, that we are their biggest fans?

Here's the good news: it's never too late to start being your
daughter's biggest fan. It's never too late to start telling her, "You
are beautiful!"

Husbands, it's also essential that our wives feel as if we are
their greatest fans as well as their teammates. It's easy for me to
fall into being just a good teammate to Chris, to help lighten
her load in life or to tackle a problem together. But she also
needs me to be her number-one raving fan.

I'm a pretty typical guy when it comes to expressing my deepest feelings. I feel things deeply, but it's difficult for me to let those feelings come through so Chris can know and feel them. I'm learning, however, that it doesn't matter how crazy I am about her or how passionately I love her if I don't express my feelings in a way that allows her to feel them.

So many times I've failed to show Chris how I feel about her. Often it has been because I struggle to share my feelings. Sometimes it has been out of complacency, and sometimes the busyness of life has distracted me from my most important role of helping my wife feel how treasured and truly beautiful she is.

All the excuses really come down to self-centeredness rather than God-centeredness. When the Holy Spirit is in control of my life, He strengthens me to do whatever it takes to let Chris feel how I feel about her. Sometimes I hear men say, "Well, I'm not good at this sharing-my-feelings thing." I certainly can relate, but it's not about what we're good at or not good at. It's about what our wives need! I have a long way to go in this area, but every time I risk the awkwardness of letting Chris know how much I love her, it fills both of our emotional tanks and draws us together as soul mates and not just teammates.

A goal I set recently is helping me show her how I really feel about her: I try to win her heart every day. Since I'm a goal-oriented guy, that little phrase—"win her heart every day"—helps me break out of my complacency with some tangible action. I imagine for a moment that Chris and I just started dating and that I better do whatever it takes today to win her heart. Some days I get her a bouquet of her favorite flowers. Other days I give her a card that tells her she's loved, or I leave a chocolate truffle on her pillow. Sometimes I just listen to her share the stresses she's experiencing, and other times I try to do something to lighten her load.

I realized that when it comes to the messages and worship services at church, I put a lot of effort, energy, and creativity into the planning. However, when it came to my relationship with Chris, I didn't put in the same creative effort to make her feel treasured. I think most of us men start coasting in our marriage relationships. The solution is not rocket science. We just need to put in the same kind of creative effort that we did back when we were dating and trying to win their hearts.

The struggle to feel beautiful begins new every day for our wives. Our part, husbands, is to start new each morning helping our wives feel what we feel about them. You can help her overcome the daily battle by making it your goal to "win her heart every day."

A GOOD FIGHT

Imagine if someone had stood up in that restaurant and said, "Excuse me, little girl, but we'd really appreciate it if you'd sit back down. We're trying to enjoy a meal here." Sure, at first it may be hard to imagine someone doing that, but think about it a minute. Yeah, not so hard now, is it? If that had happened, Megan would have needed me not to dance with her but to fight for her. She would have needed her father to defend her right to dance. What I'm really talking about is her right to be a child. Our culture loves to gush about children, but the reality is that we have little patience for children and their childlike ways. The grownup world values productivity over play, and children, at least in grownups' eyes, are not always productive.

Dad, protect your daughter's right to play, to run, to sing, to dance, to throw a fastball, to dream of building cathedrals one day, to do whatever. Help her learn, gradually, to stand on her own two feet. But in that learning process, she needs you for support, balance, and protection. If you're not there, you'll leave a hole in her life, a hole that all kinds of other things may try to rush in and fill. And most of these things are not beneficial for her heart and mind and soul and strength.

I'm not talking about fighting our daughters' battles for them. I'm talking about fighting *alongside* them, and I believe there is a difference. When our daughters are young, we need to be close, right there to defend and protect. They need to know and feel our closeness—that we are present, engaged, involved. Little girls can't articulate this need, but they know when we're there and when we're not. Our proximity as fathers lessens as our daughters grow. That's hard to swallow, but that's the way God intended it—for them to increase in independence as we decrease our presence.

Husbands, we also are to fight alongside our wives to make them feel loved and treasured. When you started dating your wife, you fought to win her. Maybe, as in my case, you had to fight off other guys! Every woman wants to feel that she is worth fighting for, that her beauty is worth pursuing.

THE CHASE

Megan and I (Jordan) began dating during our college years. She attended Baylor University, as her parents had, in Waco, Texas. I went to Texas A&M in College Station.

The story of how we became a couple is unique in several ways, and to this day I'm given a hard time about it. We grew up in the same town and attended the same church. We were in the youth ministry in our early high school years, and we were both leaders in our respective classes. We met on the beach at summer camp when I was a freshman in high school, and we picked up seashells together in one of my most daring attempts to woo a female at that awkward stage in my life.

The next semester we had a class together, and as much as I would love to say that I flirted with her every day until I won her heart, that is not true. Not only was Megan a year older than I, drop-dead gorgeous, tall, and unbelievably talented, but also her father is the head pastor of our church. This made talking to her very intimidating, so in that class, the only class we ever had together, I said merely a handful of words to my future bride.

We started to develop a relationship when our student pastor asked us to help lead a Bible study for the leaders in the student ministry. Megan didn't know it, but all week long I looked forward to that hour before Bible study that we spent prepping questions and looking up verses. That study helped me feel more comfortable around Meg, and in the later years of high school, we became really close.

She was one of my best friends, and I was one of hers. However, I wanted a lot more out of our relationship, and everybody knew it. We both had other relationships throughout high school, because she saw me only as a friend. I considered Meg way out of my league and tried to put aside my feelings for her, but they always seemed to come up at the worst time, and my other relationships suffered. Little did I know that during this time God was preparing us to be together.

After high school I spent the summer working at camps and hanging out with friends before we went separate ways for college. No relationship was as important to me as my relationship with Megan. We spent a lot of time together, and a romance started to blossom on both sides. With the summer coming to a close, I was ready to make Megan my girlfriend, but she had other plans. She sat me down and talked about how the timing was so weird and how college was a time of growth and how God would make it happen if it was meant to be (all great points), but all I heard was "no."

We continued to be great friends for an entire year, with several speed bumps along the way. I desperately wanted to be hers and have her as mine. But Megan was waiting for me to grow up a bit and pursue her the way a man should. After a particularly hard conversation, I told Megan that I couldn't be as close to her, that it was tearing me apart to see she had feelings for me but that I wasn't mature enough. So we stopped talking, texting, writing letters—we cut off all forms of communication, which was very difficult—and focused on God instead of each other.

I was able to invest more deeply in the group of believers that God had gifted me with in college, a men's organization called Brotherhood of Christian Aggies. It helped me seek out mentors and be discipled by men I respected and loved. I learned more about God, people, women, and the world in general, and when I stopped focusing entirely on Megan, God was able to truly captivate my heart and make me crazy about Him. I was more joyful than ever, thriving in my relationships with friends and roommates, learning a ton from the local church I attended, and finding depth and understanding in reading God's Word for myself. I was even making great grades (which was a miracle itself).

I learned what it meant to be respectful, to give people the benefit of the doubt, and to love them regardless of how they treated me. These lessons, I believe, helped me become a more attractive person, not just to Megan, but also to people in general.

I finished the semester by calling Megan and apologizing for being such an immature boy. I left it at that, which seemed to be exactly what she was waiting for, because she started showing interest once again. Finally, after years of being too afraid or immature, I simply asked if I could take her on a date, and she very confidently said yes.

Megan's favorite and most meaningful part of our story is that I never gave up. I knew I wanted to be with her, and even though she kept turning me down when I tried to pursue her, I never stopped fighting for her love. I didn't give up and move on, because I loved her, and I was not easily shaken. This part of our story is so important to Meg because she knows if I didn't give up then, I won't give up now or when marriage gets tough.

We both realize there will be times when we don't get along and when events will strain our marriage. But we promised we would never give up when things get hard. I didn't just promise this to her on our wedding day, but I showed her I would not give up even before we married. She knows how hard I will fight for her, and she knows I am willing to do whatever it takes to build a beautiful, lasting marriage.

Women need to know that we will fight for them. That we will do whatever it takes. That we will lay down our lives for them if necessary. We will put their wants and needs ahead of our own. We will push through uncomfortable and awkward situations and initiate conversations if it promotes a stronger marriage. We will put aside our pride and selfishness and accept responsibility for our mistakes. We are called to be the spiritual leaders of our families. That means we are to lead by serving them and meeting their needs ahead of our own. When we fight for them and alongside them, we reflect the beautiful character of Christ.

When it comes to fighting for our daughters and wives, we must also win the battle that every man faces every single day in our sex-saturated culture. It has never been easier to access pornography than it is in our society now. With one click on the computer or cell phone, images and videos appear that in years past could be accessed only by going to a seedy adult bookstore.

Men, we must get serious about this dangerous sin because nothing is more destructive, devaluing, and hurtful to our wives and daughters. It's also destructive in our lives, keeping us in a cycle of selfishness and guilt.

There is so much to say about gaining victory in this battle, and many good Christian books provide guidance for men on this subject. But we want to emphasize and encourage you with this one thing: we believe that, as men, we must humble ourselves and admit we need accountability and encouragement to win this battle. We encourage you to put a program on your computer, cell phone, iPad—whatever you use—that blocks all adult content. Also, have a close friend or your wife set the password and be your accountability partner. No program is perfect, and, yes, occasionally the program may mistakenly block a site you need. We say, however, that it's worth fighting through an inconvenience so you can win the battle over lust and be part of the solution to help women feel like the treasure they are.

BEAUTIFUL REASSURANCE

I believe Chris and Megan when they say that a woman's greatest struggle is seeing her true beauty. The question is, how can we help them see the truth?

I think one of the most important things we guys can do is keep reassuring them of the truth that they are truly beautiful. In Song of Solomon, King Solomon speaks words of reassurance to his wife:

You are beautiful, my darling,
> beautiful beyond words. . . .
You are altogether beautiful, my darling,
> beautiful in every way. . . .

You have captured my heart,
> my treasure, my bride.
You hold it hostage with one glance of your eyes.
> (4:1, 7, 9, NLT)

Four times in this passage alone he tells her she is beautiful! You're beautiful. You're beautiful. You're beautiful. You're beautiful. He's reassuring her of the truth that she is beautiful.

Men, we have a huge role to play here because we can reflect the truth to the women in our lives by reassuring them of their beauty. They're looking for reassurance. That's why they're always asking things like "Do I look good in this dress?" "Do you like my new haircut?" "Do you like this color on me?" They're asking for reassurance of the truth that they are beautiful in our eyes.

One of the worst things we can do is try to change or fix them rather than accept and love them. The culture constantly pressures women to conform to a false definition of beauty. We need to be safe buffers between them and a destructive culture.

We can create an acceptance zone where they can feel the acceptance and love of God through us. Our relationship with them should be a place where they can be their true selves and live from their sacred reflections instead of trying to live up to an unrealistic idea of beauty.

MEN CAN BE BEAUTIFUL TOO

And by the way, instead of always evaluating our wives and looking at the things they need to change, let's focus on ourselves and the changes we need to make in our character. I (Jordan) really believe that men need to work on being beautiful as well.

What makes a man attractive and draws women to him? It's not his looks as much as it is his character. Kindness and respectfulness are, I believe, the two most beautiful qualities a man can possess. These characteristics make a man attractive, or you could even say beautiful. I don't mean being kind just to a girlfriend or wife and treating only them with respect. These qualities should be evident in everything we do.

Whenever Megan and I go out to eat, I always open the door to the restaurant for her. But what stands out to her even more is when I keep the door open for the people coming in after us. It's about showing kindness and respect to everyone.

These two characteristics need to be a part of our everyday lives. Meg would not approve if I showed respect only to her and I didn't show respect to her parents or my parents. If I am not kind or respectful to my parents, or even to strangers, then how can my wife expect to be treated well by me? If that was not part of my character, there would eventually be problems in our marriage because I wouldn't be able to keep up the facade. My true self would show.

Building a beautiful character starts with those small acts and showing these qualities in all relationships, not just with your wife. Opening doors not only for your spouse but also for others, showing your parents respect, picking up trash that someone else left, and speaking kind words to strangers are just a few examples. What I'm saying is that you put others before yourself. It's not about you. It's about making sure your wife is loved and other people are loved. Then, last, think of yourself and what you want. This is how you become a beautiful man.

Some of the toughest, strongest men I know are also beautiful, because they reflect the character of Christ.

REAL VERSUS COUNTERFEIT

Speaking of real respectfulness, I (Kerry) think one of the main responsibilities a dad has regarding his daughter is to make sure she knows she should always be treated with respect and what real respect looks like. The best way to recognize if something is genuine or not is to know the real thing inside and out.

Federal agents are trained to recognize counterfeit money. Although intense study is central to their training, what is so interesting is that they never look at counterfeit money. They focus only on the real thing, memorizing every detail of the genuine article, making mental notes of each characteristic that makes it real. The thinking is that when the counterfeit money does show up, it will be easily recognizable. It will be caught not by what it is but by what it is not.[32]

Dads, we need to treat our daughters in such a way that anything other than being treasured, valued, and respected will feel strange to them. We should model for our daughters what "real" looks like so when the counterfeit comes along, they'll spot it and reject it.

Author and speaker Jen Hatmaker says that her dad always encouraged her, affirmed her, and modeled for her how she should be treated. Listen to her words:

> My dad thought me and my siblings were the most spectacular children ever born to humans. From the time we took our first breath, we were encouraged within an inch of our lives.[33]

Dads, we should be so encouraging that when our daughters are discouraged and cut down by a boyfriend, they will recognize something is terribly wrong, and they won't put up with it. We should treat them with such respect and make them feel so treasured that when a boy takes them for granted or treats them poorly, they get out of the relationship.

THE TRUE MIRROR

Let's be mirrors that reflect their true worth and beauty. Men, the only way we can do that is to look to Christ ourselves. We can't meet our wives' and daughters' deepest need to feel beautiful and to be loved perfectly. No human being can. Only God can truly meet their deepest needs, and there is only one mirror that reflects perfect love. The mirror of Christ's love.

We can, however, point our wives and daughters to the one true mirror as we look to that mirror ourselves. Megan and I (Jordan) dated for about two and half years before we tied the knot, and it was amazing to see that when God finally allowed this relationship to happen, when we were able to love each other without worshiping each other, God used the relationship to teach us more about Himself and to grow us closer together than either of us could have imagined. During those years we laughed together, cried together (which is so powerful), struggled together, and fought together—all because God had a plan for our relationship.

I remember a time right after going to the movies that Megan experienced extreme depression. She couldn't explain it, but she began to break down, and I held her but had no clue what was going on. God showed me in that moment that even though I didn't understand what was happening, I could be understanding. So we talked about it, and God used me to comfort her. He showed me that my job wasn't to fix Megan, that she was perfect exactly as she was made, that my role as her leader was to reassure her of how loved she is and then point her to the only One who can comfort, restore, and heal her.

Megan just needed to know I was there for her and I wasn't going anywhere. She didn't need me to understand her. She just needed me to comfort her and tell her that God has a plan and knows what He is doing. She needed me then, and needs me now, to lead her to God. To take care of her and make her feel secure and comforted in my arms.

The greatest thing you can ever do for your wife or your daughter is to point her to the only mirror that counts, the mirror of Christ's eyes. As you look together into Christ's loving eyes, you'll see reflected back unconditional love and eternal beauty.

But we can hear some of you saying, "Kerry and Jordan, that all sounds great. It really does. But I've not been the kind of husband who points his wife to Christ's love. I've lost a lot of days with my daughter, days when I was somewhere else doing supposedly important things. Plus, on the days I was around, I messed up more times than I care to remember. Man, I'm afraid I missed my chance." Don't worry. Just start now. The truth is, fathering a daughter never ends. Oh, it changes as she grows and has different interests. But you'll always be her dad, and because of that reality, there's always time to start doting on her. If she doesn't accept it at first, fine. Don't let it throw you. She may be waiting to see if you're serious, if you'll keep on doting or if it's something you'll do once or twice and then let it quickly pass. If you're serious about it and about her, then keep at it, no matter what. She's worth it.

Plus

Plus, and this is an epic plus, you're not alone. Take a look at this verse:

> And he shall turn the heart of the fathers to the children, and the heart of the children to their fathers.
> (Malachi 4:6, kjv)

Our heavenly Father is in the business of redemption. God delights in a father's heart being turned back toward his daughter, and it is His will that this becomes a reality. So while you may feel all alone, the truth is that God has your back, dad. God has your back, husband. Regardless of the quality of your efforts, He sees the heart behind them and will give you the strength and the compassion to be present for that daughter or wife you may have neglected over the years. When it comes to living in God's kingdom, there is always hope. It's never too late.

But just because God has your back, that doesn't mean He's going to do all the work for you. In the same way you want your daughter to learn to handle some things on her own, our heavenly Father wants us to grow in grace and wisdom, and the only way to learn is to try it. And there's no better time than right now to get started. It's not too late for beauty to begin in all our lives.

Notes

1. Catherine M. Shisslak, Marjorie Crago, and Linda S. Estes, "The Spectrum of Eating Disturbances," *International Journal of Eating Disorders* 18, no. 3 (1995): 209–19.

2. National Association of Anorexia Nervosa and Associated Disorders ten-year study, 2000. www.anad.org.

3. Public Health Service's Office in Women's Health, Eating Disorders Information Sheet, 2000.

4. Substance Abuse and Mental Health Services Administration (SAMHSA), The Center for Mental Health Services (CMHS), offices of the US Department of Health and Human Services.

5. T. D. Wade, A. Keski-Rahkonen, and J. Hudson, "Epidemiology of Eating Disorders," in *Textbook in Psychiatric Epidemiology*, 3rd ed., ed. Ming T. Tsuang and Mauricio Tohen, and Peter Jones (New York: Wiley, 2011), 343–60.

6. Patrick F. Sullivan, "Mortality in Anorexia Nervosa," *American Journal of Psychiatry* 152, no. 7 (July 1995): 1073–74.

7. Jennifer Dukes Lee, *Love Idol: Letting Go of Your Need for Approval and Seeing Yourself Through God's Eyes* (Carol Stream, IL: Tyndale, 2014), 3–4.

8. Bianca London, "Sex Siren, Flapper, Waif or Bootylicious, How the Shape of the 'Perfect' Body Has Changed over the Last 100 Years," Daily Mail.com, January 19, 2015, www.dailymail.co.uk/femail/article-2913285/How-shape -perfect-body-changed-100-years.html.

9. John Eldredge and Stasi Eldredge, *Captivating: Unveiling the Mystery of a Woman's Soul,* rev. ed. (Nashville: Thomas Nelson, 2010), 47.

10. Anita Diamant, *The Red Tent* (New York: St. Martin's Press, 1997), 1.

11. Kerry and Chris Shook, *One Month to Live: Thirty Days to a No-Regrets Life* (Colorado Springs: WaterBrook, 2008), 41–42.

12. *Strong's Concordance,* s.v. "suschématizó," http://biblehub .com/greek/4964.htm.

13. C. S. Lewis, *Mere Christianity* (New York: Harper Collins, 1952), 147–48.

14. Lewis, *Mere Christianity,* 126.

15. Leslie Leyland Fields and Dr. Jill Hubbard, *Forgiving Our Fathers and Mothers: Finding Freedom from Hurt and Hate* (Nashville: W Publishing/Thomas Nelson, 2014), 51–52.

16. Brennan Manning, *All Is Grace: A Ragamuffin Memoir,* with John Blase (Colorado Springs: Cook, 2011), 196.

17. "Malala Yousafzai," Bio, www.biography.com/people /malala-yousafzai-21362253.

18. Jason Reeves, Colbie Caillat, Antonio Dixon, Kenneth Edmonds, "Try," *Gypsy Heart,* copyright © 2014, Sony /ATV Music Publishing LLC, Universal Music Publishing Group.

19. Sergio Kletnoy, "Colbie Caillat Is Tired of Being Photoshopped: Here's What She Did About It," *Elle,* July 10, 2014, www.elle.com/beauty/makeup-skin-care/news /a14974/colbie-caillat-try-video-makeup-transformation.

20. Sharon Hersh, *Bravehearts: Unlocking the Courage to Live with Abandon* (Colorado Springs: WaterBrook, 2000), 137.

21. "They May Forget What You Said, but They Will Never Forget How You Made Them Feel," Quote Investigator, http://quoteinvestigator.com/tag/carl-w-buehner/.

22. Dominique Browning, "I'm Too Old for This," *New York Times,* August 8, 2015, www.nytimes.com/2015/08/09 /fashion/im-too-old-for-this.html.

23. "Isak Dinesen Quotes," Brainy Quote, www.brainyquote .com/quotes/quotes/i/isakdinese390738.html.

24. Sue Monk Kidd, *The Secret Life of Bees* (New York: Penguin, 2002), back matter.

25. Matthew Burnett, personal conversation with the authors.

26. Jessica Durando, "10 Inspiring Quotes by Mother Teresa, *USA Today,* August 26, 2014, www.usatoday.com/story /news/nation-now/2014/08/26/mother-teresa-quotes /14364401/.

27. "Mother Teresa Quotes," Catholic Bible 101, www .catholicbible101.com/motherteresaquotes.htm.

28. Kathryn Spink, *An Authorized Biography,* rev. ed. (New York: HarperOne, 2011), xiii.

29. Francisco A. Cruz, *The Eurasian Gentile* (Bloomington, IN: Trafford, 2014), 529.

30. Spink, *An Authorized Biography,* xiii.

31. William Beausay and Kathryn Beausay, *Girls! Helping Your Little Girl Become an Extraordinary Woman* (Grand Rapids: Revell, 1996), 13.

32. "Counterfeit Detection, Part 1," Tim Challies, Trending Topics, June 27, 2006, www.challies.com/articles /counterfeit-detection-part-1.

33. Jen Hatmaker, "Words," *Jen Hatmaker* (blog), October 19, 2011, http://jenhatmaker.com/blog/2011/10/19/words.